Loving Sophie

Lessa Clayton

Simon Publishing LLC
Naples, Florida 34114

Library of Congress Control Number: 2023920115
ISBN 979-8-9882 937-5-0 (Hardcover)
ISBN 979-8-9882 937-6-7 (Trade paperback)
ISBN 979-8-9882 937-7-4 (eBook)

"With gratitude to Lisa Binns at Second Shot (501c3) http://www.secondshot.pictures for her fantastic photos of Sophie on the front and back covers and for all the work she does to help pets find their furever families."

Cover Design by:
Robin Johnson Florida Girl Designs, Inc
www.gobookcoverdesigns.com

Printed in the United States of America

First Edition

Dedication

This book is dedicated to DJ, Gray, and Grant: my who, what, why, where, and when.

In memoriam to Merlin and King Arthur, the two sweetest Sheltie boys ever.

Table of Contents

Foreword

Never in my wildest dreams did I imagine adopting an adult rescue pit mix and then writing a narrative nonfiction book about the process, but here we are. It is a cliché to say that a person or an animal changed one's life, but there is no getting around the truth of that statement when it comes to our family adopting a dog.

Sophie is the goodest of girls, and we were very lucky to find her. We are grateful to SAAP (Stray Animal Adoption Program) in Kentucky for taking Sophie in, giving her love and medical care, and fostering her. There were many different trajectories Sophie's life could have taken once her original family was no longer able to keep her, and the fact she ended up at SAAP was the best pathway possible. We are also thankful that her original family loved and cared for Sophie the way they did. There were many things she had to learn, but good house manners and being decent to cats were lessons she already knew well.

We did not know much about pit bulls or pit mixes before we got Sophie. I knew that most pitties were usually very loving, despite their somewhat fearsome demeanor. Friends, who had pit bulls, usually showed pictures of them being house hippos or land seals. Cute dogs, who occasionally got the zoomies while wearing adorable pajamas, were all familiar. We expected something those lines and we did get that with Sophie...and a whole lot more.

While the bulk of this book is really about a very distractable family and our delusions of having life under control, there are some other themes as well. We live in a very interconnected world, and that is more obvious now than ever before. How we interact with each other matters. Erring on the side of kindness and communal care is never wrong. Our Mother Earth deserves consideration in all ways. Cats are weird and will take over the world if they ever get opposable thumbs.

Finally, a nod of recognition to all the people who rescue, foster, and adopt animals. The work can be exhausting, the expenses can seem endless, but the rewards are instantaneous and forever.

Thank you for reading. I hope you enjoy!

Lessa Clayton

One

The Meeting

I was covered in dog slobber. My body had been pummeled by the exuberant brown dog, who had practically gone through the shelter's front, plate glass window to greet us. The dog's tail was spinning like a helicopter blade and had hit us all in the face when we were sitting down on the floor to meet her. She was now rocketing from person to person in our family, absolutely giddy in the certainty that we were her people.

We were in another state, sitting on the cool tile floor of the shelter's home base located at the back-end of a slightly run down strip mall, and there was this dog. In the background we could hear the barking of other dogs, who were waiting for foster placements, and were probably very jealous because she was being given a chance. Years of animals passing through in all stages of life had made their mark on the space where you could smell the emotions of fear, hope, and resignation.

The volunteer looked at us with gentle concern. It felt like being asked to go to the blackboard and do a complicated math problem in front of the whole class, when you hadn't studied the relevant chapter yet. For better or worse, based on the pleading eyes of my tween daughter, this was our dog. Although, I could tell my husband and son were less enthusiastic.

"So, you'll take her?" the volunteer asked.

"Yes, we will take her," I said with a slight sigh. "Where do I sign?" Little did I know on that fateful evening in October 2019 how much our lives would change.

"No. We're not getting a dog."

This was a mantra repeated many times in our household. Even before my husband, DJ, and I had children, family and friends had asked when we were going to adopt a dog. Never mind that DJ was allergic to dogs or that I had spent my entire adult life living in rentals or that we both preferred cats; in the eyes of those closest to us only a dog could make our family complete. Were we somehow weird for not wanting a dog? What's wrong with preferring cats? Were dogs supposed to teach us how to be better parents? It's not like dogs had a manual on child rearing we could confiscate. Or maybe they were the weird ones, belonging to a canine cult or something. Whatever. I found it insulting that having cats was somehow not enough, and DJ was adamant that no dogs need apply for residency on the basic principle that they were too much work.

It wasn't that we hated dogs. We had both grown up in homes with house pets, and I had grown up on two different farms that also included livestock. For me, having lived in the country, dogs were there for useful purposes: to guard, to protect, and to alert. We loved our dogs, but they were free to roam the farm during the day and they came inside at night or when the weather was especially bad. They didn't require much in the way of care. Regular vaccinations and being spayed or neutered were the extent of most of their medical treatments. They didn't require much obedience training, either. They came when they were called. They wore a collar and a leash when necessary. They loved rides in the car. They would bark at, but not attack, strangers. They were friendly with our barn cats. Dogs on the farm were just part of the tapestry of daily life.

As for DJ, his allergies to dogs were part of what made him reluctant to want a dog, but he also liked quieter animals, like cats. Dogs were energetic and needed attention. They were loud and messy. While he had purchased a home in southern California in his twenties and didn't have the prohibitions against dogs that I had as a renter, he did not miss their absence in his life.

When we met and started dating, he and his roommate had two cats: Emma and Ru. Emma had been a gift to his roommate, Dave, from a former girlfriend, and Ru had been a stray, caring for kittens near their house. They had thought Ru was the kittens' mother because of the devotion shown to them only to discover that Ru was a rough and tumble male alley cat with cauliflower ears and a heart of gold. My tuxedo cat of twelve years, Max, had recently been re-homed to my parents' farm because after my divorce I could not afford an apartment in Los Angeles and have a cat on the lease. As devastated as I was by his departure, I knew that he was living the life of pampered house cat with outdoor privileges, and my parents, now on their third farm, had no dogs. Not that I should have worried about my formerly indoor-only kitty taking care of himself; he was soon lording over all the other household and barn cats.

After DJ and I were engaged, we moved in together to a rented townhouse. No pets were allowed on the lease, but we were not particularly upset because we were visiting Emma and Ru regularly as they had stayed with Dave in DJ's former house. Plus, I still missed Max. My parents might have killed me if I had gotten a kitten at that point. There are only so many pets adult children can drop on their parents' doorstep, and it was clear I had reached my limit.

Within nine months of moving to Monrovia, we got married in Palm Springs. And then we were pregnant with our first child. About four months before our daughter was born, we managed to buy our first home, a lovely Craftsman with a fenced backyard in Monrovia. The first question many people asked was, "Are you getting a dog?" We always gave them a look like they were insane for asking. For one thing, every house within a square mile of us seemed to have a dog, including our neighbor with whom we shared a driveway. His dog was left tied to the garage all day while the neighbor worked second shift at a hospital, and we always knew when our neighbor was coming home because, the little Chihuahua mix of dubious origins, would start to bark exactly five minutes before the neighbor's rusty Toyota truck would rumble up the drive. There was never any point in trying to go to sleep before 11p.m. because the driveway was right up against all the bedroom windows, and the dog was doing its own job: letting everyone know its person would soon be home.

We thought about getting a kitten about a month before our daughter, Grace, came along, but DJ talked me out of it. He rightly felt that a kitten and a newborn might be too much for me to handle, especially because I was working as a real estate agent and he was traveling out of state for work two weeks out of every month. It turns out that working full-time and having a baby are difficult activities to balance, and a kitten would not have gotten the love and attention it needed. A few years later our son, Grant, was born and three months to the day we moved from Monrovia, CA to Cincinnati, Ohio. In January. From sunny and 80 to snowing and -5 in less than twelve hours was a huge change for us all.

Our new home was much larger, and even though a toddler and a newborn were demanding, we started to have those little conversations people do where they're dancing around the topic. The conversations, held during those brief respites between diaper changes, tantrums, and meals, always went something like this:

"We could get a kitten," I'd say as casually as I could muster.

DJ looked up at me over his lasagna. His eyebrows said, "Is that really a good idea?"

"You have to admit they are the cutest."

Silence as he chewed, then he wagged a fork at me. "But they are also little and fragile. And they are nocturnal. They'll be awake all night."

I pondered that for a minute. "Grant's already awake all night."

Through bleary eyes, DJ agreed. "I know."

I wasn't done with the conversation. Other possibilities? "What about a cat?"

I was sure I was making headway when he replied, "If we get a cat, I want two pair-bonded adult females."

That was very specific. I'd always had male cats without any problems. I looked at him with interest.

"When I was a kid," he continued, "we had male cats that sprayed indoors. I don't want that."

Knowing that some battles were not worth fighting over, I had simply complied. "Okay."

We had that same basic conversation several times over that first year in Cincinnati. To be fair to both of us, we were exhausted because Grant had colic and didn't sleep at night unless someone was holding him. Grace slept like a champ, but she was an extremely busy toddler. Aside from naps and nighttime, she was a whirling dervish of activity. But the end result was the same, we had agreed to get not one, but two female bonded cats. It was just a matter of when.

I was now a full-time stay at home mom. For the first time in my adult life, I wasn't working for pay, and the adjustment was difficult. We had inadvertently moved to a neighborhood where all the other kids were tweens or teens, so our kids didn't have readily available playmates. DJ had grown up partly in Cincinnati, but after his parents divorced, he had moved with his mom and younger sister to Oregon, so his ties to the area were only from visiting his dad, stepmom, and baby sisters. I found myself in a common trap of caregivers; my days were spent with very little adult conversation.

Blogging was all the rage in 2009. Reading blogs wasn't my favorite activity, but DJ followed many different bloggers and suggested a mommy blogger, Heather Armstrong, known as "Dooce," for me to follow. He thought that since my social life had basically dwindled to seeing my favorite cashier at Trader Joe's, I might benefit from a community of people, who were all struggling with similar issues.

As luck would have it, shortly after I began reading Dooce, she started a chat board called the Dooce Community. This online community of mostly women, many of whom were mothers of young children, was a blessing. The questions asked were compelling, and the answers were usually intelligent, thoughtful, and funny. We must have caught magic because we became a relatively tight-knit group of online friends, and we became each other's support system. Being able to help each other, whether with tangible advice or a referral or a simple kind word of encouragement, made us all feel useful.

About a year after the Dooce Community formed, a well-known member asked a question about how to re-home her two cats. She'd been living in southern California with her parents, but they had sold their home and were moving to retire in the Smokey Mountains. Unsurprisingly, her parents didn't want to take her cats with them, as they already had several pets of their own moving across country. These cats were pair-bonded young adult females, and they were dependent on each other. They were litter box trained, indoor-only, spayed, had all their shots, and were friendly.

This is where I offer a "pro tip:" Don't ever facetiously agree to something because you don't think it will really transpire. In a fit of conscience because I'd been in this person's shoes, I wrote, "Well, if you can get them to Ohio, we'll take them." And thus the "DoCo Kitty Train" was born. Originally members from California all the way to Ohio offered to drive Scout and Detective Stabler from one location to the next, like a cat-themed Pony Express, but it was agreed that while the spirit of the gesture was lovely, the logistics were complicated. Imagine two cats being handed from person to person and yowling non-stop the entire 2500-mile drive across country. It's a terrifying thought. Instead, via PayPal, the cat's owner raised enough money to fly them on a direct non-stop Delta Airlines red eye from LAX to CVG. Suddenly we were getting cats.

We were excited. We made a run to PetSmart and bought litter boxes, litter, box liners, the cat food brand they already ate and liked, toys, and a scratching post since they still had their claws. What were they really like? Scout was the elder of the two, a brown tabby with a sad origin story. She'd been found as a wee kitten in the parking lot of the Santa Anita mall next to her dead mother, who had been hit by a car. Detective Stabler, a tuxedo kitty, had been adopted as a kitten and had bonded with Scout, who was about a year older.

The kids were also thrilled. Three-year-old Grace, nicknamed Gray, insisted on getting up early with me so we could drive to the airport and pick up the cats on a cold January morning. Grant, a toddler, was excited because we were excited. I worried a little bit about the kids and the cats, but cats are wonderful teachers of consent. No cat will ever do anything it doesn't want to do and trying to force a cat to do something is next to impossible.

When Gray and I arrived at the cargo bay and signed off for the cats, we received two heavy-duty carriers with two very frightened and unhappy kitties. "Let's not stress them out more," I told her. "We can get them home and settled and then they can explore." Our plan was to give them the first day or two in the playroom and laundry room, so they could adjust to being in our house, and we would slowly expand their territory as they became more comfortable.

Detective Stabler ventured first out of the carrier. We were all sitting on the floor. "Sit as still as possible, don't make many sudden moves, and let the cats come to us," I told the children. Deets, as we came to call Detective Stabler, slowly wandered over to me, sat on my lap for a brief moment, then went on to explore the rest of the spaces. Scout was shyer. DJ lured her out by using the universal language of humans with animals: a series of clicks, smooches, and pats on the ground.

Once they were out of their carriers and knew where the litter boxes, food and water dishes were, we spent a little more time just sitting there and trying to tempt them with toys and being rewarded with head butts and the occasional meow or purr. We had cats!

I, of course, rushed like a proud mama to inform the Internet. Thanks to the Dooce Community, two cats who might have otherwise been sent to a shelter and separated, had a warm, safe, and loving home together. That remains one of the most memorable moments in my life. It's joyful to see what people, total strangers really, could accomplish with determination and ingenuity.

Eventually Scout and Deets settled in and had the run of the house. The kids still slept with their bedroom doors closed, so the two cats slept in the bed with me and DJ.

Deets, who'd been the friendliest to start, became a recluse and basically hid in our room whenever the children were awake and present, only coming out at night to play, use the litter box, or eat.

Scout, however, became like Nana from Peter Pan. She was devoted to the children and followed them around, letting them play with her, dress her up, and otherwise treat her in an undignified fashion. She tolerated with excellent humor all of the children's antics. She did not, however, like adults. If DJ and I tried to pat or pick her up when she wasn't in the mood, she'd give us a strong swipe with her claws. We adults left Scout to her children and kept a wide berth.

We were a happy family of two adults, two children, and two cats. It was perfect.

Two

Asha

"Mommy, I hear a cat meowing outside." Gray tugged on me as I made the kids their favorite lunch: Trader Joe's microwave Mac and Cheese.

"You're sure Scout and Deets are in the house?"

"Yes, I just saw them."

"Okay, well it's probably a neighbor's cat. They let theirs outside." A slight internal shudder reminded me of the cat assassination of a squirrel on our back veranda that I'd witnessed a few months ago.

Gray looked up at me with big puppy-dog eyes. "But what if it's a kitten? What if it needs help?"

I sighed. The logic was irrefutable. Kittens are my kryptonite, and I certainly wouldn't want an injured cat exposed to the elements or to all the wildlife who inhabited our backyard. "Let's have lunch first and then we can go take a look."

Gray was appeased and I had some time to think. There were a couple of cats who came around and would peer in the windows and taunt Scout and Deets, but they all had homes and people who loved them. If the cat was injured, I'd have to take it to the vet and that would also mean piling the kids into the car and disrupting naptime. The more I considered it, the worse the scenario became, my imagination running wild. It was a mama cat with kittens. It was an injured mama cat with kittens. It was a feral cat that was injured and not interested in help. It was a rabid, feral cat that was injured and with rabid kittens.

After lunch I hoped that Gray had forgotten, but she wasn't a child prone to forgetting anything. As expected, she immediately began asking about the mystery cat. I gathered up Gray and Grant, warning them not to touch the cat until I said it was okay, and we ventured into the backyard. The April sunshine shone bright and welcome, though the breeze hinted of a change in the weather, and the kids were happy to be exploring our rather wild yard. Birds chirped and some opportunistic squirrels darted around searching the ground below the bird feeder for fallen and discarded seeds.

I waited a few minutes and didn't see or hear anything. "Gray, I don't think—" A cat burbled behind me. I turned around as a smoky gray cat with green eyes sauntered towards me. The kids started to rush to it and I held them back. "Please wait. Let's see if kitty is okay." I slowly approached it and squatted down. The cat immediately began purring and rubbing up against me. "She seems friendly." I did a quick scan to see if she had any obvious signs of illness or injury and found none. "You can come and meet her but move slowly and be gentle."

There was no reason to worry. The cat, who was female, was perfectly happy to rub up against the children and accept head scritches from them.

"Oh, Mommy. She's so nice. Can we keep her?" Gray asked.

"She seems like she's someone's well-fed pet. Let's give her a little more love and then we can leave her alone." The idea of a third cat, when we had finally reached a point where both Scout and Deets were fully comfortable here, seemed absurd.

"But, Mama." Grant looked at me with big, pleading eyes.

"No, it's naptime. If kitty is around after dinner, we can come back out and play with her some and maybe bring her a treat." I shuttled everyone back inside and got them down for their naps and then texted DJ, who was in Florida for the week at a conference.

He was unsurprised about our visitor. "Well, we can always get a third cat."

I groaned. That was the last thing our household needed . . . another cat.

Over the next few days, when we saw the gray kitty outside, we'd join her for a few minutes. She always purred and seemed happy to see us. She had the softest fur and the gentlest demeanor. She'd come and stand in front of windows and sort-of taunt Scout and Deets.

DJ and I were headed to Vegas for a long

weekend. My parents were watching the kids, and before we went to catch our early-morning flight I reminded them that no third kitty needed to apply for residency.

Have I mentioned my parents are cat people? They are. We returned to a cat, who now lived in our garage and was being fed twice a day. "It got cold a couple of nights ago," my mom explained by way of apology. "She goes out during the day, but she comes into the garage at night. She really is the sweetest thing. Her people must miss her."

I rolled my eyes, knowing a losing battle when I saw it. Truth be told, this cat really was sweet, the kids were over the moon about her, DJ liked her, and now my parents were feeding her. We had a new cat.

We took her to the vet and determined that she was a healthy female, spayed, about six to eight years old, not microchipped, and to anyone's knowledge, no one was looking for her. We brought her home and put her in the guest room, as it had large windows and an en suite bathroom, so we could set up a litter box and slowly integrate the new cat into the household. We took our time naming her. Some suggestions from friends were more eastern European sounding names like Sasha and Petra, but we eventually settled on Asha Greycloud. It suited her because her coat was the color of cinders, but the Greycloud was a nod to Tolkien and Middle Earth. There was something almost mystical in her demeanor, and she was a traveler well met. The vet said she was part Russian Blue, and while these are normally not common cats to see, that there must have been a whole colony of them here in Cincinnati. Many local visitors when they walked in the front door and met our new greeter, have said, "We had/ have a cat just like this one. Sweetest thing ever." Remarkable. While Scout would eventually show up and see what was going on and Deets still mostly hid from strangers, Asha was always at the door to purr and demand pets. I used her as a test of people coming into the house because if she had shied away from anyone, they wouldn't have made it past the foyer.

Unlike Scout and Deets, who really weren't sure about the feline rules of engagement, Asha had no fear and quickly brought them into line. She was dominant, yet not aggressive, with Scout and Deets, and she made it clear very quickly that this was her house too. Asha had clearly lived her previous life as an indoor-outdoor cat, and as such we would put her on a kitty harness and leash and walked her outside to explore the yard, roll around in dirt and sniff the breeze. The other two cats would look at her longingly from inside, but both were too scared to come close to the door and if we tried to pick them up so they could enjoy the world as Asha did, they would scrabble frantically away.

We were now a three-cat family, which was fine because we had four laps. We were not yet outnumbered.

Three

Clive

Trouble may come in threes, but insanity requires a fourth. I stood in front of the Ohio Alleycat Resource cages at PetSmart and stared at a male long-haired ginger named "Milkstache." It was a few weeks before Christmas in 2013, and during all of my previous trips to buy cat food and cat litter and cat toys and flea meds, the lure of the cats up for adoption had passed me by. Sure, I would stop and look at the cats, who were usually curled up and sleeping. To do otherwise would have been heartless. I would read their bios with their origin story and their personality traits, but never once had I been tempted to get a fourth cat.

Yet here I was, taking a picture of Milkstache as he stared at me calmly with a regal and disdainful expression. Texting DJ, I asked a simple question:

"Why am I not getting this cat?" He immediately replied, "I don't know. Why **aren't** you getting him?" "It would be crazy," I replied. The shrug via text could not have been clearer on my husband's side. Clearly, he was willing to abet my desire for this cat in particular.

Milkstache's bio said he was two-and-a-half-years-old. His left ear was tipped, which indicated that he had been a feral, and that was confirmed in his description. He had been a feral kitten rescued by Ohio Alleycat Resource and then had been adopted. He was described as "good" with other cats, but his original adoptive family had recently returned him as well as two of his fellow OAR rescues, through no fault of the animals. Rescues always say that, by the way, and it reminds me a little of a divorce. No fault to any other of the parties, but this just didn't work out.

Anyway, Milkstache, so named because of a small white patch above his upper lip, remained entranced with me, making eye contact and looking as if I was his only hope. Okay, perhaps that last part is a bit dramatic, but I've spent my entire life with cats, and only one other time has one been so insistent that I was its person. I got the information for how to fill out the adoption paperwork, said goodbye to Milkstache, hurriedly purchased the items I'd originally come for, and rushed to pick up the kids from school.

Once we were home and settled, I began the process of filling out the adoption paperwork. All of my pets throughout the years had either just shown up, or been given to me, except for my beloved cat, Max, who was the only pet store purchase I had ever made. Previously, standards for adoption had been relatively low: Show up, pick a pet, pay for a pet, and go home. It was shocking to read the OAR paperwork, which basically felt like an interrogation: Did we own or rent? How long had we lived in our current home? Did we have children? Other pets? What were their names and ages? Had we ever surrendered an animal to a shelter? What did we do for a living? Did we smoke? Could we provide three character references that we would be good adoptive parents?

I worked my way through the gauntlet and submitted the application. Now that we were stuck waiting for an answer, I began to imagine what life would be like with Milkstache. He was a ginger, and male gingers were known for being super chill and affectionate. He had been in a home with five other cats previously, so clearly, he didn't need to be an only cat. I was certain that he would be a cuddle bug and envisioned Milkstache sleeping curled up with the girl kitties in a big, purring pile of fur. Clearly, he would be the kids' favorite pet, and he would be a darling lap-cat. In hindsight, some lowering of expectations should have been liberally applied to these fantasies.

We were approved to adopt Milkstache. And with all the giddiness and excitement we felt when we first got the other three, we went to PetSmart to pick him up and pay the adoption fee. The volunteer there gave us a little more information about why he had been returned. According to his intake, his first family had a total of six cats, and the couple was getting a divorce, so the OAR cats were returned. I wondered if having six cats could be grounds for divorce, but the volunteer artfully eluded the question.

While Milkstache was happy to be leaving

the confines of his PetSmart cage, he was definitely not a fan of getting into a carrier, and this was very much foreshadowing. He contorted his body and used his strong claws to essentially defy physics. The volunteer eventually got him into a cardboard carrier but given the way his paws were poking out from the holes and the way his claws were trying to rip the cardboard, we were glad that the drive home was only ten minutes.

The minute Milkstache belonged to us, we began to think about names. His original moniker didn't suit him, so we took the search to the Internet and threw out the query on Facebook. There were a ton of suggestions, but the one that made us all laugh as well as suited our new pet was "Clive Owange."

I wish the story continued with Clive easily integrating into the family, but even with the slow introductions of him to the house, the people, and the three other cats, he was skittish and slow to warm up. He considered me to be his person, and it's because of his devotion to me that DJ began calling me "Treat Lady." However, Clive ran away from DJ, hissed at the children, and bullied the girl cats constantly. Whatever ideas I'd had about Clive in our lives, the reality was far different.

It took time … years … for Clive to fully settle into our home. With all adult rescue animals, you can sometimes parse out what their previous stories might have been by how they behave to seemingly normal events. For example, Clive would run and hide if he heard heavy-soled shoes walking on the floor. He was also resistant to being picked up and would scrabble away, often launching himself with his hind claws. He slowly made friends with Detective Stabler, and I'd sometimes find them sleeping together, and this friendship led to him slowly accepting DJ. Clive still bullied Scout and tried to bully Asha, who would have none of it. He required valium in order to safely get him into his carrier to go to the vet. Imagine Bill the Cat spread-eagled across your body before taking a wild jump to freedom. We often required first-aid for our wounds. The kids mostly avoided him, though by about 2016 he'd let Gray pat him and by around 2018, he stopped hissing at Grant and eventually allowed our son to scratch him behind the ears.

This eventual détente between pets and people was welcome. We would joke that we had a lap for every cat, but it truly was a good balance. We humans were relatively quiet and solitary, and the cats were much the same. Having space within the house for every entity to be by itself or with others was extremely helpful, especially for the cats. While they rarely sat on our laps, they would often perch behind our shoulders when we sat on the couch, or they'd sit next or adjacent to us. Everyone was happy. Our friends and family may have half-joked that we were "crazy cat people," but our cats suited us. Giving them a good home was a pleasure, even if joy came with a lot of cat fur and hairballs.

Four

Appeasement or Concession?

L ife defies stasis. We can wish for things to stay the same, but hearts change, whether through age or desire. The first rumblings of a shift in our household started beating harder around 2018. The kids' school had a therapy dog who visited weekly, and many of their friends had new puppies. "Look at that cute dog!" became a mantra while we were out and about, and Gray was the loudest in the family.

"My friend just got a new puppy. It is so cute," said Gray. "Can't we get a puppy?" She batted her eyes at me for affect.

"No," I said. "Your father is allergic." Silly me thinking that would nip it in the bud. Sometimes I underestimate my children.

"But Mom, there're hypoallergenic dogs. We can get one of those."

I hated to admit that I was not totally against the idea. "We could consider it, but dogs are a big responsibility. Are you willing to do the work: walk him, feed him, play with and train him?"

Gray literally jumped out of her chair and came around to hug me. "Yes, of course I will."

I tried to give her that I-know-better look. "That's what you and every other kid since the beginning of domesticating animals have said. Forgive me if I am dubious."

She squeezed me tighter and laid on the special effects. "Please. Please, please, please! I want a dog!"

I could feel my resolve melting. "We have four cats. Go cuddle one of them."

"All the cats are broken and useless. Can we get a kitten?"

I felt my eye begin to twitch. "No. I am NOT changing six litter boxes for five cats. No. No. No!"

DJ and I knew we were in trouble. No one can argue like a twelve-year-old girl, who is passionate about something she considers a matter of justice. It's not that she wore us down, but there were some changes that came with Gray entering middle school, and the imperative of having a "friend" at home became greater. There is nothing like an animal happy to see you when you return home and getting all of its devotion after a bad day of tween drama. The cats, as lovely as they were, did not offer unconditional love the way a dog would.

By 2019 it became increasingly clear that a dog was in our future, whether we wanted one or not. After the kids were in bed or when we were out on a date night, I would occasionally broach the topic of a dog with DJ. In general, he was always opposed to the idea, and I shared his opposition except that I was the one picking up unhappy children after school and helping them calm down.

"You know Gray wants a dog," I said.

DJ pressed his lips tightly together before he spoke. "We are not getting a dog."

"I hear you. But what don't you like about dogs, aside from the allergy thing? Hypoallergenic dogs do exist," would be my response as I looked at him with a wry smirk.

DJ didn't miss a beat with his quick reaction. "They're loud, stinky, needy, and slobber everywhere."

I almost laughed. "I... can't argue with you there."

"And we have cats. Aren't cats good enough?"

Who was he trying to convince, me or him? "Apparently cats aren't interested in taking walks down to our neighborhood square and getting coffee. Also, our cats are 'useless and broken.'" I made air quotes. "We love them, but they're not reliable companions."

"If we get a dog, you know we will have to take care of it," he said, taking a satisfied sip of his beer like he had just drawn a royal flush at a poker tournament.

"Gray's responsible with animals. Remember, she was lab rat captain at her school, and she did well with her hamster, Buddy."

DJ rolled his eyes and smiled with grim satisfaction. "Buddy died."

I sighed. "Only after a long, happy hamster life doing nothing but burrowing and eating carrots. We can't put Buddy's death on our child."

He gave me the adult parent look. "But you know we'll have to take care of the dog."

I wasn't ready to concede yet. "Yes. I know. And the dog will have to get along with the cats. It could work."

These conversations slowly edged their ways closer and closer to a resolution. Gray kept up the pressure. Finally, one day in August 2019, DJ caved. We could get a dog! With conditions, lots of conditions. No puppies, must be house-trained, must be hypoallergenic, must be good with cats, must be friendly with people, must be well-behaved. And must be a rescue dog.

Telling Gray and Grant that a dog was now a possibility elicited completely different reactions. Gray was predictably ecstatic, but Grant was unhappy because "dogs are loud." This wasn't a surprising response from Grant. Since he was a baby, he has always preferred quiet spaces and he has never really been fond of dogs. We assured Grant that while the dog might bark, the dog would also love him, and that dogs might be loud but they were also super fun.

Unsurprisingly, within thirty seconds, Gray was already texting me potential dogs on PetFinder. We were in the hunt for a "good dog." What we didn't know was where our search would lead us.

Five

The Search

The first few days of our PetFinder search were fun. There were so many adorable dogs, and using preferences, we could choose to see only certain breeds. The list of Poodles and Poodle-mixes was incredibly long, but it became clear that most of the Poodles available for adoption were elderly and often in need of care for chronic medical conditions. If our situation had been different, being a haven for geriatric dogs to live out their last years might have been something we would have considered because it is certainly a noble pursuit, but the strain on the cats and on DJ, and the pain the kids would experience each time a beloved dog died were too much. Plus, we really did want an active young adult Poodle.

After about a week, I realized that we'd have to broaden our search, so I asked a question about finding adult rescue Poodles on Facebook. The responses ranged from laughing emojis to prayer hands to wow faces. I was less than amused. Yes, we were looking for a needle in the haystack, but truly our goals couldn't be *that* impossible. A friend, who does wildlife rescue, suggested another friend, who worked at a dog shelter, and that took me down a long path of people politely being unable to help while they were trying not to laugh directly at me. Meanwhile, Gray was getting more and more anxious. She couldn't use her phone in school, but that didn't stop her from searching animal adoption sites on her school issued iPad and sending me multiple links via email at least twice a day.

Luckily, someone took pity on me and sent links she had found for Poodle rescues around North America. One called SPIN, Standard Poodles In Need, had the perfect dog for us. Her name was Panda and she was a two-year-old black Standard Poodle. She was leash and housetrained, good with children, other dogs, and cats, and had no other behavioral issues. Only two things about Panda were at issue: she had osteoarthritis and she was in Toronto, Canada. SPIN didn't say that adoptive dog parents had to be Canadian on their website, and naively, I didn't see how adopting a dog from Canada could be a problem. As for her osteoarthritis, it was concerning to see in a dog so young, but I consulted with dog-owners who had faced similar issues. They gave me a ton of advice about anti-inflammatory diets, gentle exercise, preferably in water if possible, and ongoing care such as acupuncture, CBD products, massage. This all seemed completely reasonable. We could adopt Panda!

Gray was super excited and somehow,

most of our friends and extended family found out about Panda. One evening, when all my after-dinner chores were done, I sat down and started to fill out the SPIN adoption application. If I had thought the OAR paperwork to adopt Clive Owange had been extensive, that was nothing compared to the seventy minutes I spent carefully detailing every aspect of our lives, why we wanted Panda, and how we could make her life better. It felt like I had completed a marathon when I hit send and then we had to wait.

While we knew SPIN wouldn't contact us immediately, we continued looking on Petfinder. It felt a little like cheating on Panda, but there was no harm in searching. Gray would email me dogs from all over the United States, until I told her to please keep her search to a hundred-mile radius. We were willing to drive to Canada for Panda, but surely if Panda wasn't available, there had to be a dog closer to home.

A day or two after the application was returned, I received an email from the woman who runs the rescue at SPIN. She explained that Panda was a great dog, but she had a chronic medical condition. Would we be able to care for her? Yes, of course. Then she asked how Panda would spend her days with us. I answered that I was a SAHM and a writer, so she would be with me most days while the kids were at school and DJ was at the office. Our house was quiet during the day and taking Panda on little walks would be enjoyable. Then she wanted to know what evenings and weekends would look like, and I told her that the kids were home then and could play with her and care for her, but I looked forward to watching Ohio State football games with Panda asleep next to me on the couch.

And that's when the penny dropped. How the woman had read our whole application and not noticed we were in Ohio is beyond me, but she was shocked to discover we weren't Canadian. The tone of the email exchange turned much cooler. No, they could not meet us in Windsor, Ontario to hand over Panda. No, they would not allow Panda to come to the United States. No, Panda would have to find a home elsewhere.

To say we were devastated is an understatement. One of the things I had appreciated about SPIN was their detailed description of each dog. They didn't stint on information, and they seemed determined to be honest in their assessment of each dog's flaws and attributes. It felt possible to adopt Panda, essentially sight unseen.

Yes, it was also silly to think we could adopt a dog from Canada. I felt like an idiot after the SPIN lady explained it to me. It's a testament to how amazing we all thought Panda was that we were willing to go to these ridiculous lengths. The woman wished me well and she later sent an update saying Panda had been adopted by a family with a farm. That was a bit of a knife-twist, but we were all happy that such a good dog had found a home where she would be loved.

We were back to square one, and it was a letdown. People would ask about Panda, and we would have to say it hadn't worked out. Of course, there were still plenty of dogs to consider, and since the individuals on PetFinder were non-responsive to our queries, we limited our searches to rescue organizations. That is where the real fun began.

Did I say fun? What I meant was pure hellscape where every rescue had slightly different rules. That wasn't so bad. Obviously different organizations have differing mission statements, and if one rescue had encountered certain problems with potential adoptive families, it made sense for them to weed out those problems before they even applied. However, one of the biggest sticking points we had was the lack of a fenced yard. We were quite surprised by this as plenty of dog-owners live in apartments or townhomes without a fenced yard. It seemed like a big middle finger to everyone who lived in a city, to be honest. Plus, we were an active family. I took almost daily walks. Obviously, those walks would be daily with a dog. The kids were full of energy, and DJ didn't object to occasionally taking a dog out. As he said, "It beats the alternative of having to clean up a mess in the house."

I cannot begin to tell you how many dogs we saw where the rescue in question would not adopt without a fenced yard. At a certain point out of sheer desperation, I would send applications, admit our fence-less sin, and plead our case for being good adoptive parents as best I could. Sadly, my efforts swayed no one.

It was beginning to feel like a full-time job, searching for a dog that we wanted to adopt from a place willing to work with us. To make things worse, I had a plaintive tween, who was constantly asking, "Did you hear from that one place?" and "Could we get this dog?" I even looked at reputable dog breeders to see if I could get an adult female, who had birthed a couple of litters of puppies and was now done at the age of four or so. The price tags gave me pause, and it felt like cheating when we were committed to an adult rescue, so that idea was pushed aside.

Because we had such an extensive list of needs, we did not look at the Humane Society. The smaller rescues were able to do more detailed descriptions of each dog's personality traits, how well trained they were, how well they got along with people and other pets. There were days when it would have been so much easier to just get a dog the way we did when I was a child. Go to the Humane Society and find a dog we liked and take it home. Unfortunately, that wasn't an option we had, so I continued the search.

There were some blips on the radar where a rescue would respond to my application favorably. One woman had a pit bull rescue in Dayton, and she had an adorable younger male pit bull, who was sweet-tempered, well-trained and a tripod. She responded to my query, and I started to get excited when she offered to bring the dog to us. We could keep him for a week, and if it didn't work out, return him. That was a no-go for me. I wanted to meet the dog first, in a setting where it was comfortable and familiar, to get a read on him. The idea of having the dog come here seemed cruel, especially if we decided not to keep him.

We were over a month into our search, and since we were looking at pit bulls/bully breeds, we had obviously expanded our criteria. Basically, as long as the dog didn't have long hair, we would consider it. Honestly, if we had found the perfect dog wandering around in our backyard and it had been a Collie or German Shepherd or Golden Retriever, we would have taken it at that point, but we had to at least attempt to find a dog that wouldn't trigger DJ's allergies.

It was beginning to feel hopeless. If someone had told me that finding an adult rescue would be so difficult, I would have scoffed, yet here we were without a dog. The idea of maybe a kitten and a sixth litter box wasn't sounding so bad after all.

Salvation came with some PetFinder links to an animal rescue in northern Kentucky called SAAP, Stray Animal Adoption Program. Our kids' babysitter, Megan, had emailed Gray with some potential SAAP dogs that fit our criteria. While she was probably tired of hearing about potential dogs every time she watched the kids, she had adopted a dog from them and she liked how they ran their organization.

We scoured SAAP's rolls of dogs. They had plenty, and they did a good job of describing the animals. Gray would email me about ones she liked and I would respond, and while we hadn't found the right dog yet, it felt like we were getting closer.

SAAP's website showed a dog named Sophera that had a picture with a Snapchat filter of a crown of flowers on her head. She had a sweet and kind face, but somewhat worried eyes. An unknown mix, short-haired, good with cats and people, dog reactive, crate-trained, and house-trained. She was four years old, spayed, and up to date on her shots. What grabbed me was the white swirl on her forehead that was surrounded by light brown fur. She looked like Goetze's Caramel Creams®.

Gray thought she was beautiful, and she made a request that I fill out yet another application. At this point, the application process could be done practically in my sleep, so I applied for Sophera. None of us had our hopes up. We were nearly two months into the search, and it felt like just throwing things at the wall to see if anything would stick.

A couple of days later, I was walking with my friend, Rebecca. She had been one of my references on all pet applications, starting with Clive Owange. Of course, the conversation turned to our dog search, and I mentioned that SAAP had received our application for Sophera and we were just waiting to hear back.

"Why don't you check your email now?" she suggested as we trudged up one of the steeper hills in my neighborhood.

"Sure, hold on." I whipped out my phone, happy for a chance to catch my breath. There was a pause in the conversation and then I exclaimed, "Wait! Rebecca! Our application for Sophera is accepted!"

We did a little happy dance right on the street and then continued walking. I could not wait to tell the kids, but first I had to reply to the volunteer from SAAP, who would coordinate our meeting with Sophera. We might be getting a dog! Arrangements were made for the next evening. Gray would have to skip soccer practice, and we would have to drive to "SAAP Station" in KY, but it was all easily done.

Gray was ecstatic when I gave her the news. Grant was less thrilled but still excited. DJ was stoic in his grim determination to be happy for the rest of us. I was just happy to be hopefully done with the process and to have Sophera be the right dog for our family.

The next evening, we were a wreck of nerves and anticipation. I had done a quick PetSmart trip earlier in the day to buy Sophera a dog food bowl, a leash, and some basic food. All we had to do was drive across the Ohio River during rush hour and find SAAP's Kentucky headquarters.

We arrived early by about half an hour, and we decided just to walk by the building and see if we could go in. The door was locked, but a light brown dog immediately hauled the person holding its leash across the linoleum floor and almost broke through the plate glass window in her excitement.

"I think that's...Sophera," I said with a tinge of wary hesitation.

"I think you're right, Mom," Gray answered. DJ and I looked at each other, and before we could decide whether we should move away from the window, the SAAP volunteer unlocked the door to let us in.

"Sorry we're early," I apologized as fifty pounds of pure muscle bounced around us.

"Not a problem," replied Heather, the volunteer, as she reeled Sophera in to allow us all to enter the building and close the door.

We did all the usual introductions and then Heather let us formally meet our dog. She was so happy to see us, so ridiculously happy. And she was wagging her tail as if she could get it to spin like a helicopter blade and levitate. She was licking us, and trying to herd us together, and bouncing from each of us like Tigger.

"What do you think?" DJ asked Gray.

"I like her!" was the immediate reply.

"So, you're taking her?" asked Heather.

DJ and I did that quick glance that parents do when they know they're defeated and possibly about to make a terrible decision but can't back out now.

"Yes," I answered firmly. "We'll take her."

Once the paperwork was done and the check written to SAAP, Sophera was settling down somewhat and I noticed a dark patch of skin on her back.

"What's that? Did she hurt herself?" I asked.

Heather's reply was quick, "No. She was locked in a shed for a few months this past spring and summer and she got mange or a flea allergy."

"Poor baby. Will it heal?"

"You would have to talk to a veterinarian. I'm not sure."

I nodded. Mange wasn't the worst thing a dog could suffer through. Heather handed me the adoption folder with all of Sophera's information and medical history that they knew, and packets of heart worm pills and flea preventatives.

"Can we name her Sophie?" Gray asked.

I was about to say she could name Sophera whatever she wanted, when Heather said, "That was actually her name before. We just changed it to Sophera because there were so many dogs and cats named Sophie here."

Gray smiled happily, clipped on Sophie's leash to her collar, and we headed to the car.

Six

Adjustments

We decided to run up 71-N to the Oakley PetSmart and pick out a dog bed and a crate for Sophie. We also got her some treats and were walking through the toy aisle to see what might be fun for her, when she spotted a thick, multi-colored rope toy that had a looped handle on one end and a tassel at the other, with rubber balls interspersed along the rope. She started to wag her tail excitedly, and when I picked up a different rope toy, she stopped wagging her tail and looked dejected.

"Oh, you want this one?" I asked picking up her clear choice, and she immediately jumped up for it.

"She wants that one, Mom," Gray confirmed.

"Yeah, I think you're right. C'mon, Sophie.

We have to pay for all this first before you play with it."

We got Sophie home and let her into the kitchen. By agreement, the kitchen was going to be where she familiarized herself with the household. We put a baby gate up at the door into the main entry and there was an easily closed pocket door between the kitchen and dining room. Sophie would have floor to ceiling windows in her alcove where her dog bed was and we would set up her crate against the closed dining room door, so she could see what was happening in the room but not be distracted by anything outside of it when crated.

Sophie bounded into the kitchen, tail wagging, and sniffing everything. I suggested that we put a leash on her and take her outside while DJ set up her crate, and the kids agreed. Getting her to hold still and put the leash back on was a task, but we eventually succeeded, whereupon we learned that Sophie had zero leash manners. It was like attempting to walk a ricocheting whirling dervish. She wove between our legs, she pulled, and she switched directions without any warning. Luckily our cul-de-sac wasn't particularly busy in the evening, so we could allow her to cavort without too much turmoil, but it was clear that she was in need of training.

She seemed happy and fascinated by all the new smells and the broad front lawns. There were definitely trees and shrubs and patches of grass that warranted closer inspection, but after doing a couple of laps, she was ready to go back inside. We gave her a light meal, showed her where her crate was, and gave her the rope toy she had chosen at PetSmart, and she settled down. The first half hour of Sophie was a victory!

The cats, however, were quite displeased by all the ruckus coming from the kitchen, and they were also annoyed because it was close to time for their "gushy" wet food, which was the highlight of their day. Asha needed the moist food to take her pill for IBS, and once we started giving her the Friskies shreds or whatever canned food she would deign to eat, Scout and Clive wanted some too. It had taken months for Deets to decide that she would not mind nice soft food either, and so now all cats demanded it in the evening before bedtime. The cacophony of feline demands, all the cats meowing and begging in their own distinctive ways, was always entertaining for everyone who wasn't me, as it was my job to get the proper cat to the correct plate as quickly as possible.

Because Clive was a bully and because Asha needed her medication, she and Scout were allowed on the island counter for this meal. Clive was re-directed to underneath the dining room table, and I had to go downstairs into the family room and yell for Deets every night. "Deeeeeets! Detective Stabler! Come on, Deets! Deets, Deets, Deets, Deets!" was the only way to get her attention and encourage her to leave our bedroom. Then I had to put the plate on the bottom step and go back upstairs and out of her sight before she would approach it. On evenings when I got it somehow wrong, Clive or Scout would get her leftovers.

This time, however, Sophie's presence had all the cats off-kilter. Asha and Scout refused to come into the kitchen, and Deets somehow knew there was an alien invader within the house and refused to leave our bedroom, and Clive opportunistically wanted to eat the entire can's worth of food. Why we hadn't fully anticipated this problem, I don't know. It's possible that because Scout and Deets had lived with dogs before and because Asha had never been bothered by dogs that we thought the integration would be simple. We soon discovered that we were very wrong.

Sophie got one more quick outside visit and then we invited her to try out her crate. Neither DJ nor I knew anything about crate training, as it wasn't a common practice when we had had dogs as kids, but Sophie was crate trained. She very easily went into her crate and settled down on the thick pad and blankets we had placed there.

"Why don't we open the baby gate so the cats can come in here and sniff around?" DJ suggested. So, we did. To our complete surprise, Clive was the first one to come into the lion's den. He seemed unperturbed by Sophie's presence and went up to the crate and sniffed at her. Then he hissed and walked away, but for Clive that seemed like a great start. The other cats weren't interested, but we left the gate open for the night so they could use the whole house as they were used to doing. Then we went to bed, exhausted by all we had accomplished in a very short time span.

The next morning was the same flurry of activity we have during the school year, though Gray woke up early on her own to walk Sophie before giving her breakfast. It felt weird to wake up to a dog in the house, like we had a guest with a language barrier. We didn't really know her, and she probably wasn't sure if this space was temporary or her actual home. It's possible she thought we were yet another foster family, just one that was spoiling her a lot. I grabbed my coffee and ate breakfast under her attentive gaze. She was still confined to the kitchen, but I was going to be with her for most of the day, so she wouldn't be lonely.

After everyone left for school and work, I did my usual household chores but with a shadow. Around 10 a.m., I got dressed and decided to take Sophie for a morning walk. It would be fun, I thought, to show her around the neighborhood. Our cul-de-sac was a part of Cincinnati that had been developed in the 1960s, and while we did not have sidewalks, we did have tree-lined streets with wide-open grassy yards. The weather was decent, sunny and calm. What could be a more perfect day to introduce Sophie to her new world?

It was with great anticipation that I leashed Sophie. We walked out the kitchen door and onto the front lawn ready to do all the sniffs, have all the wags, and maybe bark a little. My anticipatory mood should have been a hint that what was coming next would be none of the things I had hoped for, but the human ability to fool oneself is tireless.

Have you ever wrestled a bear? Been dragged by wild horses? Tried to get a feral cat into a carrier? Walking Sophie up the hill out of our cul-de-sac was like that. She pulled, she ran, she pulled while running, she wove in and around me. I dodged and weaved and got jerked to the left and forward and to the right and to the left and backwards. We had barely gone 300 feet, and I was breathing hard and in a heavy sweat. The gentle hill up to the first intersection felt like climbing a mountain. This was not the way I had imagined walking her to be, but she had to get some exercise.

At the corner of our street was a house with a large, fenced yard. I knew they had a dog, but in the years we had lived there, we had never interacted with said dog who was a black, mid-sized fuzzy thing of indeterminate everything. That changed the minute the dog and Sophie saw each other. They both got into a frenzy of barking, and Sophie was jumping up and snapping at her leash and thrashing her head in quick twists whilst dragging me closer to the fence. I was getting concerned because the intersection wasn't particularly busy, but people made fast right turns on this corner, and there was a large pine tree blocking their view. The "Corner Dog" as we eventually called it was practically frothing at the mouth, and Sophie was growling and chuffing. It's impossible to know how long this went on. It felt like years but probably only lasted five minutes, and I eventually was able to wrangle Sophie past her sworn foe and continue down the street. It took a minute for me to realize the fatal flaw to my plan…unless I wanted to walk a two-and-a-half-mile loop with this dog who was so unpredictable on a leash, we needed to walk back past Corner Dog to get home.

The walk back was one I knew well and liked because it wasn't easy. There was a steep hill and then an s-curve where the road flattened out before curving back up another hill to my street. On this walk, it felt like a marathon. It didn't help that Corner Dog was still outside, but through sheer force of will, I managed to get Sophie past her nemesis and headed home. Obviously, we had some work to do with this whole "walking" deal.

Sophie got a biscuit when we got into the house, and I flopped down at my desk in the kitchen. I definitely needed advice. The collar she had come with had almost slipped from her neck while she thrashed around earlier, and she was basically uncontrollable. This wasn't going to work, so I asked the Internet.

Luckily, I am friends with many dog people, and they universally recommended the Easy Walk® Harness. I ordered a purple sparkly one in Sophie's size and paid extra for faster delivery.

My next plan was to take her on walks where there were fewer dogs. Our neighborhood was inundated with pets of the canine persuasion, so maybe Sophie and I could go on a car ride to a less crowded park. It was the most brilliant of ideas... in theory. Much to my dismay, it became clear that Sophie's car manners were no better than her leash manners. With no one to hold onto her, she jumped from the second row to the back row, then up to the front seat, then tried to get into my lap and then back to the second row. Back and forth and through and around. This wasn't tenable. Not only was it dangerous and distracting, but also her behavior was really irritating. A quick side trip to PetSmart happened and I procured a seat buckle clip for her harness. Slowly we were making everything right for Sophie and for the rest of us.

Seven

She's a Rescue!

Because I work from home as a writer, taking care of Sophie during the weekdays fell to me. She was slowly integrating into the household. We allowed her to go all over the main level now and just had the baby gate set up at the stairs to prevent her from getting to where the cats were. While it's impossible to know exactly what the cats thought of all this noisy disruption in their lives, it's easy to guess that they preferred life without the mutt. Clive, who had been the first to meet her, now hissed at her and shied away when he came upon her, which led to Sophie looking confused. From what we knew of her history, she had lived with cats and didn't have any experience with dogs. Her demeanor was playful with the cats but also guardedly polite. She had obviously experienced a swipe or two to her nose in her previous life and knew better than to be aggressive.

Scout and Asha warily slunk around the edges of rooms, hugging the walls and darting from underneath one table to the underneath of a chair to on top of a bookcase. Asha willing came up and sniffed Sophie when she thought Sophie wasn't paying attention, but otherwise both she and Scout steered clear. As for Detective Stabler, she had returned to her behavior when she had first come to us where she mostly lived in our bedroom and only left to use a litter box or eat.

The Easy Walk Harness arrived, and I'm not going to lie, it really made walking Sophie much easier. She would still pull, but because the martingale collar clipped to her leash at the front of her neck, she felt the correction of her pulling more easily. With the harness and the seatbelt clip, Sophie and I were able to go on car rides, and one of the first places we went was the Lunken Playfield attached to Lunken Airport.

The Cincinnati Parks Department ran the recreational parts of the park. There were several softball fields, a bike trail, a golf course, tennis courts, a couple of playgrounds, and some club houses, all surrounding the municipal airport, which mostly served small, private planes. This had been a fun area to take the kids when they had been little because one of the playgrounds was well shaded and attached to a recreation building that had a snack bar and indoor restrooms. Being familiar with the layout of the park, I knew there was an enclosed picnic area that was rarely used. It seemed like the perfect place to take Sophie, so she could run around undisturbed.

October in Ohio is always beautiful, and

the day we picked was no exception. It was around 75 degrees and sunny with no humidity and that sparkle of light that you only see here in the fall months. I let Sophie into the area, unclipped her leash after closing the gate and watched her take off running like a racehorse. There were some sticks on the ground, which I tossed to her. She'd jump high into the air, twist like an acrobat, and land gracefully with the stick in her mouth. Lying on the ground and holding the stick between her two paws, she'd chew it, stopping every few seconds to look at me with a ginormous grin on her face. Much like making a baby laugh, getting a dog to smile is an exercise in purity. There's nothing more simple or more joyful.

The fenced area had several picnic tables, a few rickety small bleachers, and a huge, old oak tree. Most of the area was grassy, and with the shade from the tree, Sophie could rest easily between romping. A benefit for her was that the golf course's putting green was right in front of this fenced area, and she could watch people practicing their short game while she chewed on a stick that was bigger than she was. As for me, I could watch the executive jets and small two-seater planes taking off and landing. It was pleasant and mostly quiet, except for the dull roar of engines both in the sky and on the road.

All good things come to an end and eventually I had to put Sophie's leash back on her and get her into the car so we could pick up the kids from school, but I was happy that the proof of concept had worked. There was a fenced area where Sophie could play undisturbed.

The next big step was getting Sophie to the vet. Our veterinarian had known us since the

DoCo Kitties had arrived, so we were already established somewhere that Sophie could get trusted care. I was worried the day I took her in simply because I knew the practice mostly dealt in dogs. Truly, everyone in this city seemed to have a dog, and how Sophie might act was unknown.

My concern was for nothing. Sophie sat like a lady unperturbed by the animals around her, though some of the dogs reacted to her. This was far different than what I had been led to expect at SAAP or even what little I had seen on our walks together, and it baffled me. In fact, she was perfect for the entire visit and allowed the tech to do a thorough exam without making any fuss.

"What a good girl she is!" The tech fussed as Sophie did her helicopter tail wag and licked her all over her hands.

"She really is very friendly."

The tech looked at me. "Yes, I can see that. Her sparkly harness is adorable too."

When the vet came in, she gave Sophie a full exam, commenting repeatedly on how good a girl she was. Our cats never got that kind of praise when they were being handled by strangers, so this was definitely a change of pace. The vet finished and said, "She's very healthy, except for her teeth. We'll need to schedule her for a cleaning and most likely an extraction of some of her front incisors. Our dental vet will make the determination the day of surgery."

"Okay," I groaned inwardly. "About how much will it be?"

The vet gave me the minimum price for the cleaning and one extraction and then gave an amount per tooth after that. She said, "Don't worry. It will probably only be about $400." I nodded and grimaced.

"What about her skin back here? Will it heal?" I pointed to the rough bare patch from her tail along a third of her back.

"No, that damage is permanent. I'm sorry. She's always going be hairless there."

"Will it bother her? Will she need clothes to cover it?"

The vet nodded. "Yes, you will need to get her a winter coat to protect that spot, as it will be vulnerable to the elements. And in the summer, she will need sunscreen there. She may also want a raincoat. Rain will feel strange to her."

I smiled. "Yay! We get to dress up the dog. You hear that, Soph? You're going to be a fashionista!"

Sophie looked at me and wagged, which got her more pets.

"So, do you have any idea about her breed? SAAP thought maybe Basenji or Boxer or terrier."

The vet took a long look at Soph. "Yes. I can see all that. A DNA test would be your best bet, though. She's definitely a mix."

I nodded, thanked the vet, paid the bill, and we left without any dog encounters. When we got home, I told Sophie that she had been a very good girl and gave her a little treat. Less than a week into having a dog, and we were on top of it.

Eight

Fashionista

Sophie had a bunch of teeth extracted; all of her incisors top and bottom. She had significant gum damage, and the teeth were all loose. As a very good girl, she came home woozy and sore but in good spirits. Now that we had all the medical issues out of the way, it was time to go shopping for dog clothes. Gray, as expected, was ridiculously excited by the idea, and admittedly, it's difficult to deny the cute factor in a well-dressed dog.

There were so many options for dog clothing: shoes, jackets, sweaters, neckerchiefs, tee shirts, pajamas. Add in all the various costumes for Halloween and every other holiday in the United States, and the choices seemed endless.

What we didn't realize was that Sophie's mix of breeds made her a dog with fewer sartorial options than most. She was not a pret-a-porter type of gal. We tried with raincoats from PetSmart and sweaters from a manufacturer who specialized in pit bulls, but nothing was right. Sophie had a very long back, broad shoulders, a neck thicker than her head, a barrel chest, and a tiny waist. Imagine Dwayne Johnson's torso on Natalie Portman's hips and legs.

In frustration, I briefly considered taking up sewing again. At best, I'm a practical hand-sewing seamstress. Affixing buttons, changing hems, repairing rips are all in my wheelhouse, but at the time we didn't have a sewing machine to put together any complex patterns. Plus, there was the fact that sewing makes me itch. This has always shocked my mother, who can make anything with a needle and thread, and it disappointed my grandma, who was a seamstress by trade. Perhaps "itch" isn't the right word but my hands get hot, and I'm easily irritated just sitting in front of a sewing machine. It is a testament to my love for Sophie that I was even thinking about making her clothes.

My idea was to find an old piece of clothing and cut it down to fit her, but I didn't even have a chance to try because my mom took pity on me and offered to make Sophie a winter coat. I'm not too proud to accept help when needed, and my mom had the skills and patience necessary for the task. Gray and I measured Sophie and gave the specifications to my mom.

To say that Mom had fun with this project would be an understatement. The first coat she sent had an adorable dog bone pattern and cute pockets with fun buttons. Honestly, if Sophie had been a more sedate pup, this prototype would have worked, but we were talking about an animal who could use her shoulders to wriggle free from a collar. We sent back suggestions for improvement and waited. Eventually Mom sent a different coat with stronger buckles and Velcro to more firmly hold the coat onto Sophie's body around her neck/shoulders and waist. The Brutus Buckeye pattern was perfect too since Mom and I were both alumnae of Ohio State University, so Soph was styling. Unlike the previously purchased coats, this one was long enough to cover her entire back including the bare patch from the mange, and that was the most important part.

We had also reached a point where Sophie would give me a look at night when I would crate her. The look clearly said, "I know this is bogus, and you know this is bogus. How about I sleep in Gray's room?" So, she did. Suddenly there were dog blankets and dog beds strewn everywhere. Sophie had the run on the house when we were home. The cats continued to behave as expected, and Sophie was mostly uninterested in them, though she would occasionally try to sniff one, which meant the cat would hiss at her and scamper off to hide someplace inaccessible to dogs. As adjustments went, life with Sophie was proceeding fairly well.

Nine

"She's Not A Basenji"

One of SAAP's suggestions for Sophie's breed had been Basenji. Everyone who had owned a Basenji or who knew someone who had had one would comment on her conformation and claim it was easy to see. Basenji are known for being "bark-less" dogs. They instead make more of a high-pitched yip. Sophie had been with us for two weeks and hadn't barked when we were home. I commented to a friend that so far, we had lucked out and perhaps Sophie wouldn't bark, and the friend laughed and told me her dog did the same thing and then proceeded to bark all the time at any little thing.

Our neighbors across the street had a pair of Shelties and while they had a fenced backyard, they often took their dogs on long walks. One of the neighbors, Rick, mentioned to me that Sophie didn't stop barking when we weren't home. This concerned me because it had to be irritating for everyone able to hear her, plus it meant that she was getting riled up too much. Obviously, she could bark after all. We had dismantled the crate by now because there was no need to crate Sophie. She had perfect house manners, didn't bother the cats, didn't chew on shoes or steal food from the counters. As a work around for her barking, we decided to gate her in at the lower level, which was partially built into the hillside and only had windows facing the backyard. She wouldn't be able to see all the cars, delivery people, dogs, children, walkers, landscapers and construction workers who were a constant in our cul-de-sac, but she would be able to look out into the backyard. Therefore, she wouldn't be entirely bored.

This plan worked well, except that when she came upstairs, she'd usually bark incessantly for about five minutes as a way to acknowledge all that had happened out of her sight. When we were home and she was upstairs with us, she was quick to alert us to any change in front of the house. Nothing missed her attention, not even a leaf blowing on the walkway or a skunk scuttling into the ivy. Part of our problem was that we had large floor-to-ceiling windows in the front of the house and those windows allowed Sophie to see the entire cul-de-sac and up the street. Had our house been designed a little differently, it would have been more difficult for her to keep such a vigilant watch, but here she was afforded a broad view and there were ample distractions.

It got to the point where DJ would look at

me grimly, as Sophie barked her fool head off. "I don't think she's a Basenji," he said, and he'd stalk off to a quieter part of the house. Trying to distract her or herd her once she reached a point of extreme frenzy was not an easy task. Usually if I distracted her with a rope toy or a tennis ball, she'd stop and calm down but that didn't always work.

A trainer we had found suggested using water guns or spray bottles and spritzing her face with water when she was barking. We tried that, and honestly, if Sophie, who was the sweetest and most loving dog to her people, could have turned into Cujo, it would have been when we sprayed her with water. Her reaction honestly scared me, though we did later discover that Sophie reacted very differently to sprays of water as play rather than as a correction. She would snap, snarl, and lunge at the sprays of water. They were neither corrective nor calming; the effect was akin to attaching explosives to the tail of a dragon. She was riled up, not subdued. Instead, we continued to distract her with toys, and we would herd her into the guest room on the main level, which had no street facing windows, and close the door.

This technique worked well, except it meant we were then stuck in the guest room with the dog. While we didn't mind it in theory, in practice it meant that whatever we were doing in the rest of the house, cooking dinner, helping the kids with homework, doing chores etc., had to be put on hold until Sophie would calm down.

After Sophie went through her first course of training in February of 2020, the trainer suggested we use "calming" techniques to help her manage her anxiety. In what was necessary honesty, the trainer said, "She really hates this. I can barely get her to move." The idea was to have Sophie sit, face her, and gently make small circles with her torso. Imagine sitting on an exercise ball and making circles with your waist. It was supposed to calm Sophie, but all it did was frustrate us all.

This practice worked on other dogs, but with Sophie we were essentially trying to churn set concrete. She wouldn't budge. We'd try rotating her, and she'd just hunker into a firmer stance. It was a work-out for us just to get her to go in one circle.

Eventually we would grab Sophie in the world's most awkward hug, pat her and re-assure her as a calming technique. She responded better to this approach than the churning one, and if I narrated the event as it occurred, she responded calmly.

"Oh, look. It's the mailman. What a good girl you are to let us know he's here!"

Did she understand any of those words, except for "good girl?" I have no idea, but it seemed helpful to acknowledge that she was guarding us well while also making the appearance of the six days a week mail delivery less fraught for her. I basically used the same premise as with the kids when they were little. Narrating all the parts of their day helped develop a routine, and they knew what to expect from their days in general. Any deviations could also be explained, which gave them the comfort of knowing their parents were aware and were there for them.

Did this really work with Sophie? I believe it helped ease her anxiety simply from the fact that I was there and was calm. Sophie could take her cues from me, and as long as I was present from the beginning of the event, such as seeing the mail truck pulling up by our house, she reacted far less dramatically and settled herself faster.

Ten

"Danger Babies and Smoking Men"

Getting to know Sophie meant learning to assess who or what she might think was a threat. We learned that she had a weird sense of object permanence in that if someone was INSIDE the house with her or if she was OUTSIDE with them, she almost always was thrilled to see them. She couldn't really distinguish family, if we were outside and she was in. She'd stand up on her hind legs, resting her front paws on the windowsill and bark just as strenuously and actively when she saw us outside as when she saw a stranger. Since her barking was as animated for us as it was for strangers, it seemed like she did not quite recognize us yet. With time, she gradually came to know that we could exist outside, even if she were inside, and after a couple of years, she would just calmly wait for us to come inside instead of thinking we might be doppelgangers and a threat to her family.

Sophie loved kids of all ages, but she was overly exuberant when approaching them, which could be scary. When we could get her to sit still, she'd wag her tail with delight at meeting kids, but a lot of children, especially smaller ones, rightfully shied away from her. Once they got to know her, it was easier for everyone. I didn't blame a kid for being wary of a strange dog barreling at them, so we spent a lot of time making certain Sophie was well-behaved. No child needs to be scared by a dog. She also would be upset by crying babies and would stop on our walk with a look of concern, cocking her head in the direction of the noise. We couldn't know if she had been around toddlers or babies previously, but we could tell that she was sensitive to their upsets.

About a year before we got Sophie, a young expectant married couple moved in across the street next to our friends with the Shelties. They had an elderly black dog named Sneakers. Because the house they purchased hadn't been updated in several decades, after the baby was born, the mom and baby moved to temporary housing while the dad stayed home and managed all the sub-contractors and work done on the home. By the time the mom and baby returned, the baby was almost a toddler and we had Sophie.

Obviously, we wanted the toddler to like our dog. What we didn't expect was for Sophie to like the toddler ONLY when she was on foot and toddling around. The mere sight of the toddler being pulled in a wagon or pushed on a tricycle or settled in a stroller drove our dog crazy.

Why the baby carriage would set Sophie off, I don't know, but if she saw the baby or the carriage when they were outside and she was inside, she'd lose her mind. We took to calling the baby "Danger Baby" because Sophie acted like it was a high priority threat, up there with the mailman and UPS delivery. The funny thing was that one day we were all outside at the same time, and Sophie was able to meet Danger Baby in person instead of watching her behind glass. She was very excited and was on her best behavior. Later that day, we were inside, and Sophie saw the parents leaving with the baby carriage from the window. She went nuts, like it was a DEFCON 5 situation. Clearly the glass barrier meant one couldn't properly assess the outside, so everything was a threat again.

It was interesting how Sophie reacted differently to certain people. She was definitely drawn to men far more than women, but there was a particular kind of man she liked especially: construction workers and tradesmen who smoked. My Lord, Sophie would absolutely prostrate herself to get ear scratches from men in coveralls or jeans with work boots and a pack of smokes in their breast pocket. She would pull me so hard to meet them and after a while, I'd smile and say, "She's very friendly. She wants you to pat her." They usually obliged. Yes, training protocol was being broken, but one learns to pick one's battles after being dragged across various lawns and roads.

Luckily, aside from one telecom worker who wanted no part of meeting her, everyone else indulged her. She'd have the biggest grin on her face, and her tail would be pure helicopter, and she'd lick them like they were made of gravy.

"I love dogs," one said chimed in with, "she's a beauty."

"I've got a dog just like her at home," another said. He stroked her head and she practically purred. "Where'd you get her?

"She's a rescue," I'd say, proud that we persevered with the whole rescue criteria we'd been so set on. If the conversation progressed because no one's schedule was pressing and the weather was fine, they would notice her damaged skin on her back. I'd have to say she'd been previously abused and gotten mange. The men would always tut sympathetically. Once Sophie had gotten her fill, we would continue along on our walk, and she would have a little jaunt in her step.

I had taken to finding relatively quiet trails in the area where we could hike. Partly this was because I enjoyed being in the woods, but the other more important benefit was that we could walk undisturbed by other dogs. Sophie could sniff to her heart's content, and I could take pictures of interesting tableaus. It was perfect.

Every woman or person perceived as somehow vulnerable will understand my other reason for enjoying these walks with Sophie. Walking with a dog like Sophie made me feel safer. I had grown up deep in the Hocking Hills of southeastern Ohio and had spent plenty of time alone or with friends tramping around in the woods without any supervision. This was an activity that I missed, and the fact Sophie made it possible again was wonderful.

However, given Sophie's love for men,

I was beginning to question how she would behave in a situation where a man might be threatening. Hopefully, she would know the difference, but aside from her barking from inside the house at the outside world, there were no indications during in-person meetings that she had much discernment. The only real distinctions she made were socioeconomic. She had much less interest in the tennis-golf-squash-fit men running or walking in our areas compared to men in work boots who smoked. But even the men with country club memberships were greeted with tail wags and a happy face.

One evening, Gray and I were walking Sophie. It was dark and cold, probably late November. As I stopped to pick up Sophie's poop, I noticed a man walking around the curve and something about him seemed not quite right. It's hard to say what made him seem questionable. Plenty of people walk in our neighborhood at night. He had a headlamp, like for mining, on his head and he was dressed all in black but none of that was overtly suspicious. Still, he made me nervous.

Because I did not want to relay my fear to Sophie or to Gray, I purposely slowed my heart rate and continued talking to Gray as if there was nothing wrong. I finished picking up after Sophie a few seconds before the man passed us on the other side of the road, and it's a good thing the situation had my full attention. Sophie went ballistic. She leapt in the air several feet, barking, growling and lunging toward the man. She was absolutely losing her mind. Gray and I got her under control as the man continued apace up the hill and away from us.

"Mom."

"I know."

"That was crazy."

"Yeah, but now we know that Sophie can tell the difference. I didn't like that guy."

Gray nodded. "I didn't either. I'm glad we were out with Sophie."

We started to walk back home, which was the same direction as the man had been walking. Our street didn't have sidewalks, and I had drilled it into the kids since they were toddlers to always walk facing traffic. Unfortunately, a lot of the people in our neighborhood or passing through were unaware of this simple rule, and I was always mildly annoyed to see people being oblivious because of the dangers involved.

As we walked, we stayed quiet and kept an eye on the man ahead of us. When he continued into our cul-de-sac, I tilted my head at Gray to indicate that we were dodging down the cross street. We didn't want him to know where we lived.

The world women live in is one where we have to constantly be vigilant about our surroundings. I'm not saying that women need to carry a weapon or stay home or only travel in packs or stay with men for protection, and it's also true that men also can find themselves in dangerous situations when out alone. However, the calculus that women make in public life is far different than how men interact in public. When I think back to that evening, it's highly doubtful that the man was up to anything nefarious. Yet our dog wasn't impressed by him, and he struck both me and my daughter as being somehow "off." Luckily to date that has been the only incident where Sophie has not been enthusiastic about meeting another human, and it is when

I started to truly trust Sophie as a companion. We eventually got home once we were certain that the cul-de-sac was clear. DJ wanted to know what had taken us so long, and when we told him, he was grateful that Sophie had been a very good girl. We all were.

Eleven

Enemies of the Street

Any dog can be reactive. It's not a breed-specific trait. The way they respond are all different as well. Sophie was leash-reactive, meaning when she was leashed and came across another dog she tended to lunge and bark.

We lived in a neighborhood filled with dogs. Some had fenced backyards, and we only heard them. Others were behind electric fences and would run up to the boundaries and either bark furiously or simply wag their tail in pleasure. Many dogs, however, were walked regularly. Eventually we got to know some of the dogs and owners by sight, though it was rare that we could stop and chat.

Early on in our walks, we kept passing a very kind looking woman with two English Setters. The dogs seemed completely chill, and

Sophie expressed a lot of interest in meeting them. Her tail would wag happily, and she would have a bounce in her step. When I one day asked if they could possibly sniff each other, it was a disaster. They all immediately started a kerfuffle, and I pulled Sophie away apologizing profusely.

After I got over my initial inclination to put our house up for sale and move far away, Sophie and I worked on how to deal with other dogs. The biggest thing that worked was getting her to sit on a short leash. I would talk to Sophie, rub her ears, tell her she was a good girl and talk about the other dogs and people in a sing-song voice. "Look at that cute fluffy puppy! Don't you love its pink leash? Maybe we can get a leash like that for you, huh?"

When we first started this technique, Sophie would literally shake. She'd emit a low growl and would look like she was ready to lose her mind. Luckily, over time she became used to the routine, and now she either sits quietly or even lies down. I know! We didn't tell her to lie down! But I wasn't about to argue with the reactive rescue dog when she's doing the right thing even without the right command. In the time we've had Sophie, the owner of the English Setters and I can now pass each other with our dogs, exchange pleasantries about the weather, and keep moving without any drama.

What I could not control were the other dogs we saw. Usually, leashed dogs were not an issue, except for smaller dogs on long, retractable leashes when they had boundary issues. Where we struggled was with larger dogs behind electric fences and with unleashed dogs. For example, one beautiful spring afternoon we were in the process of taking Sophie outside for a late afternoon pee before dinner. Sophie was leashed, but our neighbors across the street were in their yard playing fetch with their two Shelties. Their dogs are well-trained and not overly reactive, but on this day, the younger dog saw Sophie and sprinted through their lawn, across the street, and into our driveway to have vigorous "words" with Sophie. Neither dog was injured, but Sophie was rattled. We had one more incident like that before our neighbors decided to play fetch in their fenced backyard. I felt bad about that because we really enjoy our neighbors as friends, and both of the Shelties (Arthur and Anna) are adorable. Whatever hopes I may have had about puppy "play dates" with Arthur and Anna and Sophie in Rick and Richard's lovely back yard with the in-ground pool, koi pond, and large shade trees, it was clear that we would have to find other outlets for fun.

Before getting Sophie, dogs behind electric fences always gave me a little pause if I walked by their houses and they came sprinting up to the boundaries of their yards to bark at me. It wasn't that I was really concerned that they would break through, but it could be startling to have a dog suddenly appear without warning. After getting Sophie, my feelings on dogs with electric fences changed drastically. Too many times dogs have broken containment from their electric fences and gone out into the street. Often it appears that the dogs have been left outside for too long and have become agitated. They feel the need to guard and alert, but they are not getting any necessary down-time away from all the sensory inputs of the outdoors, which causes them to over-react. Once a Miniature Poodle ran from its open garage and down its lawn and across the street to attack Sophie, which was rather hilarious because Sophie was nonplussed. She had this look on her face, like "Is this for real?" Another time at the other end of the street, Sophie and I were walking and a larger dog, who was loose in his yard with supervision from his human, decided to take off and come sprinting up the hill about 200 feet. Luckily that dog was a bit out of breath after the exertion and nothing dire happened.

Everyone's been apologetic and kind. These incidents are part and parcel of dog ownership. But does Sophie give off some sort of hormonal vibe, which aggravates other reactive dogs? With not knowing much about her history, I have noticed that she has a small divot in her right ear just at the tip. It's possible that as a puppy, she had an incident with another dog, and that is why she's wary of dogs. We know that she lived in a home with at least one teenage boy and several cats. She hadn't been spayed before being rescued by SAAP, even though she was about four years old when they took her in. She also had never been pregnant or birthed puppies. My guess is that she didn't have regular contact with other dogs and this was part of her animus, but there is no real way to know for certain.

Before the COVID-19 pandemic hit the United States in March of 2020, we had just finished training with Sophie. She had done an intense four-day, three-night "boot camp" with a highly regarded local trainer. Afterwards, we had a few individual sessions because a dog is only as well-trained as its people, by which I mean all people need to give consistent instructions to the dog. Having the whole family present to work with Sophie and the trainer was really useful.

The trainer offered group classes for re-active dogs, and we were getting ready to sign up for those once we were back from our annual spring break vacation to Florida. However, we needed someone to take in Sophie for the week we were gone, and unfortunately the trainer was booked for boarding into July. The trainer recommended that I look on *Rover* for sitters as there was no way we could leave Sophie at home alone with the cats. While the cats would have someone coming in daily to feed them, give them their medicine and play with them, that person lived on the other side of town. Asking her to stay at our house for a week was out of the question because she was in the midst of all the bridal activities for her April 4th wedding, which was rescheduled to September that year for pandemic reasons.

I was starting to panic, but the Rover app seemed really straight-forward and easy. What we wanted was someone who had a fenced yard and understood dogs like Sophie. There were plenty of people who billed themselves as "dog experts" and who claimed reactive dogs were no problem, but when I spoke with them and talked about Sophie, they showed hesitation and inexperience.

Luckily, we found one couple who had a fenced yard and multiple dogs. The husband worked from home, so there would be ongoing supervision, and they had a spare bedroom set up for the "guest" dogs, so Sophie could sleep there undisturbed. Their rates were reasonable, and they were willing to meet Sophie, and have her meet their dogs.

I'm not going to lie; I was worried about a potential blood bath. My imagination ran wild with images of Sophie attacking their dogs and being aggressive. The day we went to their house was a beautiful Saturday in March, and I was wondering how big a vet bill this visit might entail.

They lived on a quiet street in a neighborhood a few miles away from ours. We came up to a cute Craftsman bungalow and rang the doorbell, immediately hearing dogs barking in the back of the house. The owners let us in and met Sophie. I was incredibly worried because the humans seemed like really nice people, and the idea of having to clean up blood from a dog fight in their living room that was started by my dog made me queasy. Sophie was on her best manners with the humans. She liked them and they liked her. We also liked them, so the initial part of the interview was stellar. I explained that SAAP had informed us that if she had slow introductions, Sophie did well with other dogs, so they brought out a smaller dog first. It was an older terrier and weighed about fifteen pounds. Sophie stood there stiffly, and it seemed like she was experiencing anxiety. The little dog walked all around her, sniffed every bit of her its nose could reach, and then licked her. It was that easy.

Amazed, we watched the couple's other dogs come out slowly and greet Sophie. She was off leash and happy and relaxed. The dogs liked her, she liked them, and they were soon romping around the living room like old pals. It was crazy. DJ and I looked at each other like we were dreaming. Where was the reactive dog losing her mind at the sight of other dogs? This was an easy-going animal we had never seen before. Maybe it was a territorial thing. Sophie knew she was in their territory, so she accepted that. And they were obviously trained to accept other dogs into their territory.

The pet sitters agreed that Sophie would be no trouble, and we arranged for dropping her off in a couple of weeks' time. Unfortunately, because we were visiting family in Florida and because the pandemic started ramping up and everything was closing, we canceled our trip and didn't need the services of the pet sitters. We did allow them to charge us because we all knew everything was going to get really weird. What we didn't know was that a year later, we would still be in this holding pattern of waiting out the coronavirus.

The virus also changed how Sophie's training continued. Instead of meeting for in-person group classes, the trainer offered Zoom classes. Since Sophie's biggest issue was reactivity to other dogs, the Zoom classes were not something that seemed useful at the time. We decided to build on what she had learned from the trainer and continue working on her public demeanor ourselves instead of participating in the Zoom classes.

Twelve

Don't Lick Me

Sophie was settling into our household with relative ease. She now slept with Gray in her room. When we weren't home, she went to the lower level and would hang out with the cats. When we were home, she'd follow whichever one of us was the most interesting, i.e. had food, snacks or was willing to play with her. She soon became a frequent companion curled up next to us when we were sitting anywhere she could squeeze herself: Beds, couches, over-sized chairs, chaise lounges. All resting places were fair game.

The cats were getting used to her. Asha was the first to offer acceptance when one night she got up on the chaise lounge where Sophie and I were and sat at the other side of my feet. This became a habit of either Scout or Asha sharing space with Sophie, even if they weren't exactly cuddled together. They would only do this if we were present.

Often at night before bed, DJ and I would hang out in the guest room on the main level. He would sit in his Plycraft chair with his feet on the ottoman and I'd lounge on the bed. We'd often have at least two cats with us, and before Sophie came along, it was possible that all of the cats would join us. Sometimes DJ and I would sit next to each other on the bed, catching up on TV shows on the iPad, and we would be surrounded by all the cats, who kept a sharp eye on us before bedtime because they didn't want to miss out on any of their treats.

The addition of Sophie changed the equation a bit. She was beginning to feel safe with us, and she was a very affectionate dog. I didn't mind being licked to death, but it turned out that DJ's dog allergy was more to saliva than fur because the first time her tongue hit his face, he had an immediate reaction. The part of his cheek that Sophie had licked turned red and immediately became itchy. Sophie would want to show us her love and would be giving me a tongue bath and then would turn to DJ, only for him to sternly hold up a hand and say, "Don't lick me." It became a running joke. He would play tug of war with her or rub her belly or toss a ball to her, but the minute her tongue came out, he backed away.

Everything was becoming easy again in that slow, gradual way that seems imperceptible at the time but puts the past in a hazy glow. It's funny how human beings remember huge changes in their lives and how things that were overwhelming in the moment often turn out to be funny in the re-telling. It was on a Friday or

Saturday night, as these always seem to be, when Sophie did something she often did, bark at whatever was in the street.

We had taken to giving Sophie chews. They weren't rawhide, but they were a similar animal by-product that gave her something of a challenge to eat. This particular evening, she was lounging in the front entry and working diligently on her chew when some pedestrians walking a dog happened by. Sophie reacted as usual, but this time her barking started mid-chew and she began to choke.

Choking, she stumbled to me, her eyes wide. She could breathe, but she was in distress. I opened her mouth and felt around to see if there was any obvious obstruction, and there was nothing I could see. So, I did the next logical thing and performed the Heimlich on my dog, which is really not an easy feat. Sophie seemed in less distress afterwards and the choke was an occasional cough, but it seemed prudent to go to the vet.

Of course, just like human beings always need a doctor at the most inconvenient of times, so do pets. 9 p.m. on a weekend night meant that our beloved regular vet wasn't available, so Gray and I geared Sophie up, helped her into my car, and drove her to the emergency vet. Luckily the emergency vet is relatively close to our house, and we were able to get there quickly.

It felt like forever. Time is mutable in these situations. A minute can feel like a year and an hour can feel like a few seconds. We rushed to the vet, parked like a stunt driver, ran into the waiting room and breathlessly explained Sophie's situation. The vet techs were all very compassionate and professional. They took Sophie back for an exam while we filled out paperwork. That seemed odd because we wanted to be with her, but we knew she was in good hands. Once we had completed everything, Gray found a vending machine and demanded money for a soda. Normally I wouldn't comply with that kind of request, but my defenses were weak and handing her a couple of dollars calmed us both down.

The waiting is always the hardest part, as Tom Petty astutely noted. We sat with other pet parents looking at each other with sideways glances. Most of the people sat quietly, just stoically waiting to find out when they could return home with their pet and how much the bill would be. A few people were visibly upset, but they moved over to the other side of the large room, settled on a couch, and made themselves comfortable for what presumably would be a long night.

After thirty or forty minutes, we were called back to an exam room. Sophie wasn't there, which immediately worried me, and Gray gave me a look that shared my fears.

The vet came in a minute or so later with a smile. "There's nothing to worry about. Sophie is just fine. We'll bring her around in a minute, but could you tell us a little more about what happened?"

We walked her through it, explaining the chew treat, Sophie's habit of being deranged at the sight of anything moving out front, how we had noticed she was in distress, and what we did to help her.

The vet nodded sagely throughout. "Those chews are going in the trash, right?"

We assured her they were, though I was feeling a little put out at this point. We were responsible pet owners! How could we have known a branded pet chew would cause her to choke? We didn't buy rawhide for her; didn't that count for something?

Luckily, the vet didn't seem interested in castigating us for the incident. Her focus was on making sure we didn't have this trouble again, which was entirely fair. No one wanted to be this stressed or see Sophie hurt in any way. The entire ordeal had highlighted the fact that we were all very fortunate that Sophie would be coming back home with us, happy and healthy. The vet gave us after-care instructions, told us they would file a report for our regular vet, and advised us to call again if anything changed. It was all very easy.

When the tech brought Sophie into the room, you would have thought we were having a reunion after not seeing each other for years. She was so happy, her tail spinning. Gray and I were in tears, just giving her huge hugs. I texted DJ, let him know Sophie was still alive, and that we were coming home. Then we paid the bill and blessedly were able to leave.

Sophie got a hero's welcome when we arrived. Grant and DJ met us all at the kitchen door, and she ran in and licked everyone. DJ immediately went to the sink to wash his hands, but instead of being annoyed, he just laughed, "This is the one time she can lick me after that trouble. Tomorrow it's back to normal."

Here is where the differences between cats and dogs become apparent. When cats are injured or sick, they want to be left alone. In fact, they will rarely "tell" their people they aren't feeling well and this results in vet visits where every possible test has to be run to determine what's wrong.

Dogs, however, are quick to make it known that they need help and Sophie was no exception.

Thirteen

C.U.C.A.

Training helped Sophie a lot. She could sit and stay on command. She had a good down. She would walk on our left when leashed. All of this was a gradual progression over about a year or eighteen months. It's also true that a dog's training is only as good as the person enforcing the rules. In this regard, we were intentionally a bit lax.

With the absence of a fenced yard, Sophie only interacted with the outside world on-leash, with the exception of the times we would take her to an enclosed area. Sophie loved to sniff things. Everything. Anything. Technically, we were supposed to keep her moving and not allow her to be distracted by the larger world, but she took so much visible joy in smelling certain flowers, shrubs, and trees that it was difficult to deny her.

As a compromise, we'd let her get a lot of sniffs in until she'd had her first poop, and then we would rein her in a bit. On walks where she had been in the same places several days in a row, getting her to keep moving was much easier, but any time we varied the walk routine, we were back to square one.

Sophie's sensitive nose combined with her gremlin-like ears meant she was always on alert. However, familiarizing her with the regular neighborhood smells helped her be less reactive to dogs she saw more often. We began to joke that there was an organization for dogs called the Canine Urination Club of America, and members could discern each other by sniffing frequent pee sites.

This approach to dealing with Sophie might make experienced dog trainers cringe because we were doing it "wrong," but I would argue that Sophie's happiness counted as much as her behavior. As an avid walker and hiker, I'm a big advocate for people exploring their worlds at a walking pace. We miss so much when we breeze by in a car or even a bike. One of the things we had done with the kids, once they were toddlers, was to take them out of strollers and have them walk with us. Their core muscles strengthened. They got more physical exercise and thus took better naps. Most importantly, they got to stop and explore the world at their leisure. Every parent does things a little differently than everyone else, and this was one area where we were definitely unconventional.

The one problem with letting Sophie stop and sniff everything was that her terrier instincts would kick in and she would start to dig in the dirt. This was less of an issue when we were walking in the woods, but our neighborhood prided itself on exquisitely manicured lawns, except for our house, which really was an outlier in horticultural standards … a polite way of saying we had dandelions. It was too rude to allow her to dig a hole to the center of the world in someone else's lawn, so we had to quickly teach her to find something else to do instead.

Sophie's finely-tuned nose extended beyond dog urine. She could smell changes in the weather and more than once on a day where the forecast was just for some clouds, she would abruptly turn around mid-walk and trot quickly back home. In those instances, I at first tried to keep going because I had no idea what she was communicating to me, but it quickly became apparent that had she been human, we could have gotten her a job as a meteorologist. Once we understood her methods, she prevented us from getting soaked a couple of times, as we would get to the house just as a major downpour started.

Fourteen

The Shadow Year

A couple of months after we adopted Sophie, news started coming out of China regarding a mysterious illness that was making people very sick and killing an unexpected number of people. Shortly thereafter it was discovered that the illness was a novel coronavirus, named COVID-19 by researchers. At first, we were not terribly concerned. There had been outbreaks of Ebola and SARS and MERS in the past decade on other continents that had not affected us in the United States, and since not much was known about this virus, it seemed to be something we would keep an eye on yet not have our lives disrupted entirely. We were wrong.

I am not sure how to describe the panic that people felt once it became clear that COVID-19 was becoming a global pandemic. Scientists and medical professionals were scrambling to figure out exactly how the virus acted on the human body and how best to prevent the spread of the virus while still caring for those infected. There was a ton of information that hit us all like a tsunami: the virus was airborne, the virus was transmitted through physical contact, the virus stayed active on surfaces for days, the virus didn't live longer than an hour outside the human body, the virus could be contained by masks, the virus could not be contained by masks, certain vitamins and herbal supplements protected people against getting sick, animals could pass the virus to humans, only elderly people died and so forth. Only some of this information was accurate and a lot of it was a partial truth or an observation made from incomplete data. We felt wrung out after trying to parse a deluge of news and determine how seriously to take the pandemic and what steps we could take to reasonably prevent it.

In March of 2020, it became clear that the virus was in the United States, and the concern was that it would spread too rapidly for communities to handle. Out of an abundance of caution, many states "closed down" in order to keep people home and to prevent them from adding their bodies to the virus's goal of continued spread. Ohio was one of those states. Our Governor, Mike DeWine, took the virus seriously, and he closed all non-essential businesses and closed all schools. We were grateful for the guidance, but then we were faced with other new concerns: how to maintain the kids being in "virtual" school while still keeping up with household chores and how to make certain we had enough supplies and food for everyone in the household while supply chains around the globe were being stretched practically into non-existence.

The maintenance of the kids while in virtual school wasn't too complicated on its face. The school was able to quickly pivot and use new technology to provide for a classroom "experience" online. However, it was tough to find places for both kids to be where they could comfortably be in class yet we would not be interrupting them or vice versa. For Gray it was relatively easy. Her room was big enough to have a desk that she had repurposed into a vanity, but it was a space where her iPad would fit and she had a comfortable chair. In Grant's case, his bedroom was too small for a desk, so we couldn't put him there and he spent the entire spring quarter wandering around the house from room to room, like a disgruntled ghost. This wouldn't have been a problem, but it meant that everyone else had to know when and where he was in order not to interrupt him.

Another issue was Sophie and the cats. All the animals were used to it just being me home all day during the week. While Asha and Sophie loved all the extra attention, Clive, Scout, and Detective Stabler were clearly put out. Their routines were being disturbed and that was wrong, as they let us know constantly. We also had to keep an eye on Sophie, as we couldn't let her stand at the front window and bark for even a second if Grant were online in the kitchen, dining room or living room. This meant that we had to be constantly vigilant about where Sophie was in the house during school. The best option was to keep her on the bedroom level where Gray was and where DJ was working from his home office. We could close the gate at the stairs, and Sophie would be oblivious to anything happening elsewhere unless the doorbell rang. Another option was to keep her in the guest room off the living room with me to keep her company. This option was fine for short stretches, but she got bored if she spent too long in the guest room and I would get antsy because being there meant I wasn't getting anything else done.

I won't lie; the first months of all this were tedious. Not only were we trying to get masks so we could leave the house, but we also were all dealing with the shock of the situation. That said, we coped. If one grocery store didn't have milk, another one might. When bread shelves were empty, eggs were plentiful. No French toast for breakfast but a frittata for dinner was easy.

We were also lucky. The kids had access to iPads and reliable Internet service, so they could stay home. DJ's office shut down entirely and put everyone to remote work. As of this writing, the kids are back at school in person, but DJis still able to work mostly from home. Many of the hassles, inconveniences, fears, and worries faced by others were not ones we shared directly, though we were incredibly upset at the ways the pandemic upended people's lives. It was common for us to check in with our friends, who were medical staff or service workers and were "essential." In fact, we discovered as a country that no one was more essential than the employees working at 24-hour fast-food restaurants because whether you were getting off a hospital shift at 3 a.m. or hauling your rig across country to deliver much needed supplies, driving through and getting a hot meal meant the world.

In terms of continuing to train Sophie, we

were less fortunate. Her doggie boot camp had finished, and we were supposed to start her in group classes when the pandemic hit and everything shut down. Eventually group classes did resume online, but I learned early on that I disliked online platforms for doing group work, and everything was so stressful that adding to my stress wasn't necessary. Besides, the whole point of the group classes was based on Sophie becoming better socialized and less reactive to other dogs. A class on Zoom simply didn't make any sense.

So, we ended up training Sophie in sort of ad hoc, trial and error approaches. To our surprise, it mostly worked.

One of the things I believe firmly as a parent is that consistency is key. We carried that over to how we dealt with Sophie. If she was at the front windows and started to bark, we first taught her to pick a toy. She would do so, shaking it violently as she watched the interlopers dare be in our cul-de-sac. This approach had merit, but when Grant was online at school, he found her theatrics to be distracting, so we taught her the word "Go" and would point at the guest room. That meant she needed to go there and wait for us to join her. At first, she took it as an opportunity to find a different toy or saw it as a game of chase where she would go into the guest room, see us following her, and then she'd sprint out of the room past us and back to the front windows where she could express herself more fully. Eventually however, after months of telling her and then showing her what to do, she got it.

We would also point downstairs and say, "Go" in a firm tone, and she would reluctantly take herself down the stairs, her long back swinging in three different directions as she did. Once downstairs, she would look mournfully over the baby gate and chuff expectantly, but if we ignored her, she would finally sigh and wander off to DJ's office or Gray's room to lie down.

Learning all of these commands and following them took a lot longer than we would have liked, but our patience did pay off in that Sophie learned what was and wasn't acceptable. She is always a work in progress, but it turns out that with time, you can teach old dog's new tricks.

Fifteen

Saying The Quiet Parts Out Loud

"You're not allowed to be in there!"

Sophie and I were back at Lunken. It was late August or early September, and the kids' camp was finished. The sun was bright, and the day promised to get hot, but right now we were shaded by the large oak tree after playing a rousing game of fetch with an old stick.

I heard someone speaking.

"Excuse me?" I said, turning to see an older woman on a golf cart.

"This is private property. You can't be here. There's a dog park on the other side of the airport. You have to go there."

I walked towards the woman and got a

closer look. She had just finished her round of golf and was alone. If I had to guess, she was a retiree because people who work are rarely on golf courses at 10:45 a.m. on a weekday. Had I been smart, I would have taken out my phone to record the conversation, but it honestly didn't occur to me that this woman wouldn't take me at my word, which I realize speaks to my relative privilege in life.

"We have permission to be here. It's okay," I said as I reached the fence.

She frowned and scoffed, "Who told you that it was okay? This is private property! There are children's camps here!"

I nodded, trying to show that I was listening, "The camp director told me —"

"What's her name?" she interrupted. Then she began to huff, "You don't know the camp director! This is private property! All of this …" She swept her left arm to indicate the tennis courts, driving range, golf course, and picnic area where Sophie and I were. "… is private. You have no right to be here."

Sighing, I shook my head, "No. I spoke to the camp director in May. We avoided coming here because she mentioned that there would be kids using this area over the summer, but they're in school now. We have permission."

"Why are you here with **that** dog?" she rounded on me.

"What? It's a fenced area. She's playing," I indicated to Sophie, who was on the ground in full splort and was chewing on a stick between her front paws while tentatively wagging her tail at the prospect of this new human being possibly giving her pets.

The woman scowled and then frowned, "That dog is a menace."

"What?" I sputtered, utterly confused as to how Sophie's current demeanor could indicate anything other than a happy and well-behaved dog.

The woman nodded with a smirk, "Oh, I can tell. I can always tell. That dog is no good."

Now I was irritated, "Why would you say that?"

"I can always tell. Dogs like that are trouble."

"Dogs like what?" I asked with a dangerous edge to my voice.

"Like that," she said contemptuously.

"Ma'am, are you attempting to breed shame my dog?"

"I don't have to. I've raised and trained more dogs than you'll ever know and that kind of dog is trouble," she sneered.

"Okay, well, I'll send a memo to the AKC that brown mixed breeds are trouble. Will that help?"

"Do what you want, but I'm going to send the golf course manager over here. He'll tell you!" She sped off, as fast as one can speed off, in her golf cart.

The interaction left me flustered and stunned. I walked outside the fenced area and checked the sign. It clearly said Cincinnati Recreational Parks. There were no signs prohibiting dogs. I had spoken with a park employee at the beginning of the summer, and she had been amenable to us using the space in the months when summer camps were not happening. People had seen me show up with Sophie for months before that and no one had ever said a word. It was bizarre.

While I waited for Brad or Steve or Jason or whoever was supposedly the golf course manager to show up, I took a video of where we were and detailed what had just happened. Now I was ready for a fight. I even Googled the park and confirmed what I already knew; all of it, including the golf course, was public property. In addition, while other parks had camps for kids running into autumn, this park was done with that program for the year.

Sophie continued to play, oblivious to any drama surrounding her, as I triple-checked everything and gathered my thoughts. One of the woman's objections had been that Sophie would "defecate where children play," but we were always careful to pick up after Sophie and throw away the poop bags in the garbage can near the tennis court parking lot. And we were outside in a public space that had birds, rats, squirrels, raccoons, deer and all sorts wandering through without a single care and yet the idea of a dog dropping a load outside had outraged this woman.

After about fifteen minutes with no sign of any officious looking men approaching us, I put Sophie's leash on and we went to the car. It was so irritating what this woman had done. She had made so many presumptions about Sophie with absolutely no information to support it. In fact, she had told lies in an effort to cow me into agreeing with her. I texted DJ, got into the car, and drove home with Sophie happily in the back seat, looking out the window and catching the breeze on her face. It wasn't until later that day, when I relayed the events to a friend and they asked if I had recorded it, that the penny fully dropped. Sophie had been "Karen-ed."

The cultural phenomenon of a "Karen" isn't necessarily new, but the name for it is. My apologies to people named Karen because every single one of you I know is a lovely and caring person, but the cultural zeitgeist has spoken. Essentially a Karen is a white woman, who is unhappy with something or someone innocuous in her environment. That part isn't so new, but with the advent of camera phones able to record these interactions, the world has seen how Karens are not innocent in how the scenarios play out. There are hundreds, if not thousands of videos, where a white woman has lost her mind because Black people were barbecuing in a public park or because a store employee has asked her to put on a face-mask during the pandemic. The lists of activities that a Karen finds offensive are endless, but the crucial dynamic is always one where the Karen feels justified to exert her authority over someone she believes isn't as powerful or important as she is. Very rarely does the Karen in question have any real authority and even more rarely is the victim of her outrage doing anything wrong. The crux of what the Karen perceives as her advantage in the power dynamics, is usually based on race or socioeconomic factors.

It had taken me aback to realize what had happened because rarely are any of my activities called into question. My appearance in the world is that of a relatively middle-class white woman, who is middle-aged and appropriately bland. I'm boring. I'm usually boring on purpose and that's okay. Being innocuous is camouflage. I'm not the droid you're looking for, and even if I were, you wouldn't think I was.

So, being harassed by a complete stranger when I had done absolutely nothing wrong was an entirely new experience for me. Truly, my goal on this earth is to leave it better than I found it. In my opinion, the sad fact is that because of the racism in our country, my interactions are rarely under scrutiny because my whiteness acts as a shield. Unfortunately, Black, Brown, and Indigenous people in the United States don't have the same unearned privileges of being able to exist freely in the public eye. Thanks to Karens and their ilk, my encounter with the angry white woman, while rare for me, is all too common for anyone who isn't white.

This led me to the realization that Sophie is not a "white" dog. She is not a dog you will find in my neighborhood or around it. She is a mutt. She is a rescue. She has a bare patch of skin on her back from mange. She looks a little like a pit bull, even though her muzzle is narrower, her head isn't quite as blocky, and her torso is slimmer. It's the fact about her looking like a pit bull that really makes her suspect and causes her to stand out like a sore thumb on walks. Our neighborhood is one of pure-bred dogs or acceptable mixed breeds. I wonder if we mixed a Poodle and a pit bull together, what would we get? A poot? A piddle? And would that mix be deemed appropriate? It is hard to say.

The fact is Sophie is a dog that you expect to see riding in a pick-up truck with a gun rack or in a low-rider that has big fuzzy dice hanging from the rear-view mirror. With her short legs, long back, big ears, barrel chest, thick neck, dainty waist, pretty face, and helicopter tail, she's uniquely herself, but we live in a world where pedigree can matter. Much like there is status associated with what university one attends or what car one drives, the animals we choose also make a statement. I don't want to place a value judgment in any case. Our choices in life are as much about luck as circumstances. Sophie was lucky to live the first part of her life with a family, who loved her deeply. She was in rough circumstances for several months when she was housed in a shed. She was lucky to go to SAAP, an organization that is dedicated to rescuing animals, and not the pound. Her circumstances changed when she came to live with us, and we were lucky to get her.

Sixteen

The Inevitable Shift

Those of us who have been kids, all of us, and those of us who are parents, some of us, are familiar with the dynamics of asking and getting. In almost all circumstances, the parent eventually has to take on some of the kid's responsibilities. Sometimes that is no fault of the kid; there are a million reasons why kids cannot always take full care of their pets. Any sensible adult entering into one of these bargains with a child has to realize that some of the pet's care will need to be met by them, not the child.

With Sophie, it was obvious from the day we got her that I would be responsible for her primary walk during the school week. The kids couldn't ditch class, come home, walk her, and then return to school. Even if they had been able to drive themselves or were within walking distance of home, there would not have been enough time to properly care for the dog's needs.

This state of affairs was fine by me most of the time. While it took weeks and then months and then almost a full year before Sophie and I could walk around our own neighborhood without incident, my patience with her was rarely shaken. As I've mentioned, it didn't bother me if Sophie stopped to smell some flowers or inspect a rock. This was her walk. If it took us twice as long to go the same distance I could walk by myself, that was just the price to be paid.

Where things began to unravel was that Gray's initial enthusiasm for her dog began to wane. Oh, she loved Sophie just as much as ever. Her face would light up when she came home from school and Sophie was there to greet her, wagging her tail and spinning herself dizzy in circles. Sophie slept with her. Sophie looked to her. Sophie played with her. But the thrill of having a dog was somewhat diminished by the reality of having that dog.

DJ and I expected Gray to walk Sophie on the weekends, but she was hitting that stage in her development when sleeping in on the weekend was essential. Getting her up and moving wasn't impossible, and she would happily walk Sophie once she was properly awake. However, Sophie didn't always want to wait until 10:30 or 11:00 a.m. for her second foray outside when other people, namely me, walked her at 10 a.m. during the work week. That meant that either DJ and I walked Sophie together or one of us took her out by ourselves.

About this time, we began to frame Sophie as a perpetual toddler: she had a very particular schedule with at least four forays outside and lots of playing and plenty of naps. For some reason, we felt less resentful of the added responsibility of a dog when we thought of her this way. We had lived through the toddler stage of two children, and at least Sophie didn't require play dates. This framing also helped DJ sort-of fall in love with Sophie. He saw how happy she made me, and how much I loved her. When he saw her as not really more complicated than a small child, it was easier for him to accept that Sophie was Sophie. A reductive position but it created a scenario where he was less annoyed by all her "dog-ness" and actually enjoyed spending time with her.

Having DJ begin to truly like Sophie was immensely helpful. A lot of tension dissipated. She still couldn't lick him, but he happily played with her, let her curl up on the couch next to him, and generally gave her all the consideration of any other beloved family pet.

At a certain point in Sophie's tenure with us I made the very firm mental decision that our home was it for Sophie. Part of this was simply the fact that the process of acquiring a dog had been so fraught that the idea of returning her and trying again seemed ridiculous. However, a much larger part of my decision was learning how much upheaval Sophie had already experienced. Once I realized how much she had already been through, it was clear that she was our dog, we were her people, and she was going to get all the love and care she deserved.

I also noticed that the longer Sophie lived with us, the less anxious her expression was. It took her at least six months not to have this vaguely worried look in her eyes, like "This is nice, but will the next thing be good too? When does the bad thing happen?" That really broke my heart. All dogs have one mission in life: pleasing their people. The fact that Sophie probably thought all the moving from loving initial home to dark garden shed to animal shelter to multiple foster homes to us was a sign she had "done something wrong" was too sad to bear. Yes, I am most likely anthropomorphizing her, but there was no denying that the longer she stayed with us, the more comfortable and confident she became.

It was while we were adjusting to Sophie in our lives that Gray became less interested in her. This led to several conversations like this:

"It's time for you to take Sophie out to pee before dinner," said DJ.

Gray grunted. "Can't you do it? I'm busy."

DJ put on his no-nonsense face. "No. She's **your** dog."

Gray would grudgingly move along and take care of Sophie, but she was resentful. To be fair to my elder child, the kids were going through a lot at the time. Middle school isn't easy for anyone, and the toll the pandemic took on our spirits was undeniable. We were all limited in our social activities out of necessity. Movies were streamed instead of seen in the theater. Dinners were no longer at restaurants but were carried out and brought back home. Food cooked at home required recipe changes because the supply chains didn't have every ingredient available for shipment and purchase. Going to the gym seemed like a plague pit, and the mall was not much better. Add in the fact that school was virtual for a while and when it was finally held in person, everyone was masked and kept several feet away from everyone else. The casual interactions of middle school were far less common.

Gray was in a funk. She was grateful for Sophie, but she was not caring for her. Despite all our warnings, they had thought only of the fun parts of bringing a dog into the family. This was to be expected, but it did not have to be tolerated.

One day, we sat her down for a little chat. She knew something was up because in general, her grades were great, and she did well in school and was a lovely kid in many regards. It was rare that we had to ask her to discuss anything with us.

"So Gray," I said. "Let's talk about your dog."

"Sophie?"

I resisted an eye roll. "That's the one."

DJ looked at me over Gray's head. "That's the **only** one."

I cleared my throat, giving DJ some side-eye. "Let us be blunt, Gray. You're not taking good care of her."

Gray fidgeted a bit, not looking either DJ or me in the eyes. "She is a lot of work, Mom. I don't always have time."

DJ leaned in a little closer to Gray. "You knew going in that a dog would be work."

"Yes," said Gray meekly.

I reached for her hand. "We knew going in that you wouldn't always be able to do everything for Sophie, especially because we don't have a fenced yard."

Gray looked up at me. "Yeah, and—"

"And, knowing that is no excuse for dumping so much responsibility on us."

Gray's shoulders slumped and she slid a little lower in her chair. "But she's so difficult and she's kind of dumb."

I could see DJ trying hard not to smile. "She's a dog. That's exactly what dogs are."

This time I couldn't resist the eye roll. "Gray, she is **not** a difficult dog. You have no idea how good she actually is. Your father and I grew up with dogs. We can tell you some stories."

DJ, warming to the idea of telling stories about awful pets said, "Yeah, one of our dogs used to snack off of the used cat's litter and then vomit in the living room."

"Right," I said nodding emphatically. "And my Pekinese, Honey, would eat horse manure out in the pasture and then vomit it up in the kitchen."

"That's gross." Gray wrinkled her nose.

"Yes, it is gross. Dogs can be gross," I said. "Sophie, however, has lovely indoor manners. She doesn't chew on anything she isn't allowed to have. She doesn't steal food off of the counters. She doesn't steal food from the cats. She is really far better with the cats than they deserve considering how they treat her. She's house-trained. She's…"

Gray sighed heavily. "But she's really hard to walk. I wanted a dog I could walk to the Square with and get coffee and have the dog be all cute and happy, not acting like a deranged lunatic every time a dog walks by or trying to lick all the people to death because she loves them so much."

DJ tried his best at a sympathetic but unyielding smile. "We know. But this is the dog you have. This is the dog you begged for. This is the dog we got after a lengthy and exhaustive search where your mom filled out countless applications. For you. Because you wanted a dog. Welcome to having a dog."

"I **know**, Dad. Jeez. It's just not what I expected."

"No, it isn't, and I am sorry," I explained. "But Sophie loves you so very much and she's a part of this family now. She's a really good dog. She's not perfect, but she's our imperfect dog. And we love her."

Tears glistened in Gray's eyes. "I love her too, Mom. It's just…"

"Expectations and reality didn't match?" DJ asked kindly.

Gray nodded. "Yeah."

I sat up straighter, determined to resolve this problem. Isn't that what Moms do? Clearing my throat, I said gently. "We will do our best by you and by Sophie. I would suggest, however, that you see what is great about Sophie. There's far more that is wonderful about her than is annoying."

Gray looked at me, mouth gaping open. "Mom! She's destroyed your car."

"Yep," I said. "And in three years, it will be the car you drive to school. Maybe by then her car manners will have improved."

I'd been hoping for at least a small chuckle. I should have known better. We had to have this conversation or a one similar to it a couple of times before it sunk in for Gray. It could be easy to be annoyed about them, and one might construe she was acting like a spoiled brat. I may have had that thought once or twice during this process. However, this was a child who only knew purebred dogs or designer mixed breeds prior to Sophie. No one we knew had a mutt, everyone had a fenced yard, and the Instagram and Snapchat life of dog ownership did not tell the whole story. The lesson I hoped Gray and Grant walked away with was that expectations and reality are not always on the same page in life. How one manages to cope in situations that aren't perfectly curated is part of resilience.

Once everyone was in their pandemic "bubble," Gray started having sleepovers at our house and going to her friends' homes. When Gray was home, Sophie slept in her bed. I'd find them in the morning, Gray's long limbs stretched on her twin bed with Sophie cinnamon-rolled alongside her. When Gray invited friends, all the girls would use our guest room. It had a queen bed, a large, carpeted floor, and an en-suite bathroom. In an advantage for the rest of us, it was on the main level of the house. The girls could stay up as late as they wanted, bake brownies in the kitchen at 3 a.m., screech in faux-horror at whatever they could find streaming on the Roku, and we would be blissfully undisturbed. They also had Sophie, which she loved. All of Gray's friends were super kind to her, and she thrived at being the center of attention.

When Gray had sleepovers away from home, Sophie slept with Grant in his bunk bed. This would displace Scout, who would usually come and join me and DJ and Detective Stabler. Somehow, Sophie seemed to fill Grant's room and bed far more than she did Gray's. I don't think that was the most comfortable place for her, but Grant loved having her join him. He had not been particularly fond of Sophie when she first arrived, but with time, he had grown to enjoy her. The benefits of Sophie were rooted in the fact that she loved her people, and we were her people. That big smile, that helicopter tail, that enthusiastic presence were all aspects of Sophie that made her dear to us.

Seventeen

Gone Visitin'

I could hear my mom drawing her breath in over the phone. "So, you're bringing Sophie?" she asked.

"Yes, we are. If that's okay." My fingers were mentally crossed. While Sophie would be just fine staying at home with DJ and Grant, Gray and I were her people. Bringing her would ease a certain amount of anxiety for everyone, and it would lessen the load in terms of chores my husband and son would have to do while we were gone. Plus, Gray was bringing a friend, and the friend loved Sophie. She would have three days of ample outdoor space in which to romp around and lots of adoring fans to play with her and give her cuddles.

I could tell Mom was making various mental calculations, so I stayed silent.

"Is she quieter?"

"Yes."

My mom paused. My parents had not seen Sophie since December of 2019, minus a brief five-minute visit in December of 2020 where they had driven down to bring gifts. Sophie had been so very excited to see them. Wag, wag, wriggle, wriggle, bark, bark, jump and lick. It was clear that they didn't know how much progress she had made. Then again, I wasn't sure how much progress she had made either because it felt like always a little improvement and then a back slide. Still, she was a far different dog than the one we adopted in October of 2019.

"When Sophie was there for Thanksgiving a month after we got her, did she damage anything?" I asked.

"Oh, no. She was very good," Mom answered quickly.

"Okay, so if she didn't damage anything, what is the concern? What am I missing?"

Mom paused. "Well, she is just so much. She can really barrel through a room."

"Yes, she can," I acquiesced. "And if you don't want her to come, that is fine. She will do great with DJ and Grant."

"No, no. She can come."

Hesitating I asked, "Are you sure? I don't want you to be inconvenienced."

"Yes. I am sure. It will be fine."

It turned out that my father needed to have a hip replaced, which happened three weeks before we were due to arrive. Because of the surgery we would have to be extra careful with Sophie and make sure that she couldn't bump into him as she could easily knock him over. Meanwhile, my parents hosted my Uncle Jack and Aunt Ruth Ann a few days after his surgery, and my mom insisted that it had been easy. She did, however, report that Dad was having some partial hip dislocations and his surgeon was thinking about re-doing the surgery.

That decision was accelerated one day about a week before we were supposed to arrive when Dad was in his workshop and his hip totally dislocated. An ambulance run to the hospital and an emergency hip replacement the next day ensued. My mom and I chatted often, and she was insistent that everything would be fine. Dad came home the next day and aside from having to deal with two major surgeries within a short period of time, he was active and feeling better. The trip was happening.

Monday dawned hot and sunny. DJ took Sophie for her morning walk, so I could get the car loaded. When they returned, Sophie was panting like she had run a marathon. "Soph, come here. Have some water." We called to her, trying to tempt her before the long trip. She drank a little and ate some of her breakfast, but it was clear that she knew something was up and she was too amped to settle. I had packed water and a bowl for her, so when we stopped for lunch, she could rehydrate more then. Gray and her friend piled into the back seat with Sophie between them, and we set off for northwestern Ohio.

The car ride was easy. It was the day after Independence Day, so most people were on holiday and the roads were clear. We made it up to the Piqua Dairy Queen around noon. Sophie must have recognized the destination because the minute I pulled into the lot, she began this high-pitched whine. I parked and helped get her out of the car. Gray took the $20 I handed her and didn't really listen to my order, but she went in with her friend Charlotte while I walked Sophie around in the grassy area between the restaurant and the main road. Because the DQ dining room was still closed due to the pandemic my worry had been the difficulty of finding a table outside, but it appeared that everyone was opting to eat in their cars, so we had plenty of choices.

I went into the courtyard, put Sophie's leash around a chair leg, and poured her some water, which she gratefully lapped up. The kids came out a few minutes later with the food, and we ate as fast as we could. It was ninety degrees, and there was no shade. None of us, including Soph, like hot weather. We fed her some fries and I gave the kids more money to get ice cream, while I got back into the car and ran the A/C for Sophie. She was starting to settle down after all the excitement in the morning, and my hope was that she would nap the rest of the way.

Once the kids were back, we were off again. About an hour and a half later we arrived at my parents' farm, and Sophie woke up, realized where we were and lost her mind. I had asked my parents to keep Dad inside and to give Sophie a few minutes to run around first, but the minute the car stopped, they were both coming out the front door. Visions of ambulances and ER visits danced through my head, but before I could articulate my fears, the girls were out of the car and freeing Sophie from her car harness.

Nothing happened. Sophie barreled around the yard and she took a ginormous single leap up onto the porch, by-passing the four steps, but the minute she saw my father, she came to a halt and was as gentle as a lamb. This shouldn't have been a surprise, really. Animals are often sensitive to not only the emotions of people but also their physical ailments. It just seemed unlikely that Sophie would be that aware, as she always appeared to operate from a place of pure id.

We all settled in, and the girls and Sophie wandered around outside to inspect everything. The field next to my parents' property had wheat being harvested, but the harvester had broken down in the middle of a row. The farmer was working on the machine and of course, Sophie needed to see what the deal was. She and the girls introduced themselves and then continued to explore. Everyone was happier to have open land underfoot and a wide sky above, and Sophie was very well-behaved off-leash.

That evening over supper, we planned out the activities for the next couple of days. Mom and I wanted to make a foray to Grand Rapids, a little village on the Maumee River. Gray was familiar with the offerings of all the quaint little shops, and Charlotte was excited to see what all the fuss was about. However, Mom wanted my father to join us. The idea seemed ridiculous. It was going to be about 95 degrees outside and while Grand Rapids wasn't a huge metropolis, it did have a solid two blocks of stores and restaurants. The thirty-minute drive to the village and then the two hours spent shopping seemed like too much for Dad, and he agreed, but my mom was adamant that he not be left alone.

"Goddammit, Terry Gail. I'll be fine," he grumbled as we cleared the table.

I tried to hide my smirk because I knew he

was going to say those exact words, as my mom responded as predicted, "But Thomas, what if something happens? You'll be all alone here…"

"He'll have Sophie," I interrupted. "Look, she's not Lassie, but I'm sure she would protect him if necessary."

"That's not the point, Lessa. I'm worried about him going up and down stairs."

"Goddammit, I'll be **fine**," my dad growled.

I shrugged, trying not to laugh. "He says he'll be fine. He's an adult. If he promises to stay on one level of the house while we're gone, that should be okay. Right?"

Mom hesitated, "Well…"

Dad harrumphed. "I don't need to stay on one level in my own house. I have things to do!"

"Oh, Thomas," said Mom. "What on earth do you have to do?"

"I don't know, but I don't want to not be able to do them."

I sighed. "Look, Dad. Just tell her that you'll stay on one level. And if you do go up or down, don't fall and break your hip or die because no one is feeling sorry for you at this point, okay?"

"Okay, fine."

There was a brief silence, and then my mom burst out, "This is not fine!"

"Mom, I get it, but he's old enough to make this decision. He knows the consequences. I will point and laugh if he ends up in traction after we warned him not to. We can go with the girls, and Sophie can guard Dad."

"Okay, fine."

I poured us all some more wine and sat back, satisfied that none of this would be a disaster.

The next day was predictably brutally hot, but Mom, the girls, and I set out for Grand Rapids and had a lovely time nosing around antique stores, independent booksellers, and shops filled with locally grown or made products. We even hit up Rita's Custard at the end to sit in the shade and eat frozen treats before heading back to the farm.

All was quiet when we returned. Sophie came downstairs to greet us, and my dad wasn't lying crumpled at the bottom of the stairs. Mom went up to check, and he was taking a nap in bed.

It wasn't until we were getting ready for dinner when the first hint appeared that something was awry. I asked the girls to take Sophie out for her pre-dinner walk and told them to take the leash. They found the leash and found Sophie, but they were unable to find Sophie's collar. We spent about fifteen minutes looking all over the inside of the house when I finally told the girls to put on her travel harness and use that, and then I went downstairs to help Mom in the kitchen.

The girls and Sophie went out, and my mom and I got the table set. She was just calling Dad to come down to eat when the girls came back in with Sophie's collar in hand. "Look what we found!"

"Where was it?" I asked.

"Outside by the porch on the lawn," Gray replied nonchalantly.

"Oh, really? Huh," I said.

Just then my mom walked into the kitchen.

"Guess what? The girls found Sophie's collar."

"Really? Great! Where was it?" she asked, as she turned down the burner on the ratatouille.

"Outside," I replied with a slight twitch of my lips.

She paused and turned slowly. "Outside? How did it get outside?"

"Well, given the unlikely scenario that Sophie suddenly grew opposable thumbs, it seems that Dad took her outside."

Her mouth dropped open. "What? Thomas would never. He's been upstairs this whole time."

I gave a slight shrug, as my dad walked into the kitchen.

"So, Dad. You went outside with Sophie, right?"

He looked at me with big, innocent blue eyes. "Of course. It's nice out in the shade, and I wanted to smoke a cigar. Sophie was very good. How did you figure it out?"

I laughed. "She shook off her collar because her neck is bigger than her head. She ratted you out, Dad."

Mom banged some pans around and huffed, "Thomas! You promised."

Dad looked her straight in the eyes. "It was the only way to get you to go out with the girls, which is what you wanted to do."

"Well. I just…thank goodness you're okay." Mom went back to her cooking, and I opened a bottle of wine for us. The evening settled down, but my mood was greatly improved. All my life, I had heard my mom say, "Thomas would never!" and it was glorious to see her proven wrong in real time.

Eighteen

Dog Days

The girls and I returned to Cincinnati without incident, and once home, our summer became an onslaught of contractors, appointments and shopping trips to home improvement stores and design centers. By summer, I mean *my* summer. DJ did do some of the heavy lifting, literally in terms of moving furniture around so work could be done and figuratively by dealing with everyone when I'd had enough 'peopling' for one day, but in general all of the design decisions and appointments with various subcontractors and such were handled by me. DJ would get debriefed and could override a decision, if necessary, but the details of the projects and scheduling of appointments fell to me. We were both happy with this arrangement, except that being on "contractor time" meant our carefully curated schedule was more like a hot mess of moving timelines. On very hot days, I took Sophie to the park with the fenced picnic area and large shade tree. On very rainy days, we took speedy walks around our neighborhood where she would stop every few feet and shake the water off and then look at me like it was my fault. The best way to describe a picture of Sophie's face in the rain was "hang-dog."

We went back again in August to visit my parents' farm, this time for my father's birthday. Sophie did well staying within the boundaries of my parents' property, though she really loved running around the now empty hayfield. Even with its furrowed soil and clumpy shards of stalks, it was a magical open place for her. We'd go for walks out there, and she'd sprint happily from one end of the field to the other. Dad's hip replacement was healing much better the second time around, and he was more active. He even drove us into Toledo one evening for dinner at a well-known Lebanese restaurant. Seeing him more active was a relief because both my parents pride themselves on being capable of doing anything they wanted without needing to ask for help. They were miserable even contemplating the idea of simply sitting and doing nothing all day, though I sometimes think it would do them a world of good to be a little lazy.

Once we were back home, it was the same drill again. I felt bad because Sophie had really enjoyed her time off-leash at the farm and in an area without other dogs to distract her. She did well and followed voice commands. Unfortunately, neither DJ nor I trusted her to behave well under normal circumstances. She wasn't a bad dog, but the peanut brain would short out. You could practically see it happen on her face as her expression changed, and she tried to do whatever impulsive, incorrect thing she had in mind. It was our job to do our very best to prevent those impulses from gaining traction.

During this time, we had two separate contractors working on our house. The interior painters were tasked with working on the bedroom level and painting several bedrooms, a hallway, and a couple of bathrooms. They would greet Sophie every morning, and she'd wag her tail and be happy to see them, but it was imperative to keep her out of that area while they worked. We even had to corral the cats, which meant they only had several other rooms where they could pointedly ignore each other, but they now had to face THE DOG and there were fewer beds available to hide under.

Needless to say, we were all a bit out of sorts during this stretch, but then the exterior painters showed up, and everything was right with the world, if you were Sophie. She adored the exterior painters with a passion I can't quite explain, and they adored her right back. Because we were going through a big heat wave, they would arrive at 6:30 a.m. and leave for the day at 2 p.m. Sophie would hear their ladders clanging, and she'd push her way out of Gray's room and barrel up the stairs, insistent on greeting everyone before they started work. Pats and wags were exchanged, and then we would spend the day wrangling all the animals so that none got out of an open exterior door. The painters would let Sophie hang out on the veranda in the back and let her sniff everything. Luckily, she didn't knock any paint cans over or step in any roller trays, and once her curiosity was satisfied, she would go back inside and settle down.

It was at this point when our training equilibrium took a hit. Sophie and I were walking home after a routine morning outing. As always, I was on high alert for any dogs being walked or out in their front lawns with electric fences. A few days before the event that was about to unfold, a dog at the other end of the street had gotten out of its yard and charged up the hill about a hundred yards to greet Sophie, but luckily neither dog had been hurt. I don't think that dog was serious about inflicting injury; instead, it seemed more determined to show dominance and then leave when its person arrived.

This time, I was tired. It was hot outside, and I had not been sleeping well in the guest room. The bed was smaller, so DJ and I had a difficult time being comfortably arranged. The guest room was also brighter and louder than our bedroom, so I could hear things like our neighbor's garage door going up and down. I mentioned all this because I was exhausted, my guard was down, the day was already getting unpleasant, and we were almost home. As always, I had scanned the house at the top of the cul-de-sac for the enemy Golden Retriever, but he wasn't out front that day. Because that house was the terminus for another street and at a T-intersection, the goal was to avoid being hit by any cars while also not creating a scenario where Sophie and this dog could interact.

We had just gotten beyond their front shrubs with no sign of the enemy dog, when I heard a guttural growl and he ran from behind the house, up their driveway and out into the street to very emphatically attack Sophie. Our trainer, when I mentioned these situations to her, had advised me to get between the two dogs and to let Sophie know I was protecting her. Believe me when I say I tried valiantly to get between the two, but the Golden Retriever had about twenty pounds on Sophie and Sophie was pure muscle. Sophie did not so much attack the dog as defend herself, but the defense was definitely toothy.

The dog's owner heard me yelling and ran up to grab his dog, pulling him away.

I was covered in dog hair and cranky. "This is the third time your dog has broken his electric fence. Stop this."

My neighbor was apologetic and asked me if Sophie was all right.

"I don't know. I need to get home and calm her down." And me. Sweat was pouring off of me, and I had to keep wiping my eyes to see clearly. He offered to pay any vet bills, and I demurred. "I don't think she's seriously hurt, but this is ridiculous. We have to walk by your house to leave the cul-de-sac." I pulled Sophie away, as she now wanted to go another round, which I'm sure she would have lost, and we went home.

Sophie was injured. Not badly, but the Golden Retriever had drawn blood and bitten her ear. We had an annual veterinary visit scheduled for a few days later, but we called our veterinarian and asked to come in for a check of her wounds. Sophie sat in the kitchen, wagging her tail and bleeding. We attempted to calm her and eventually convinced her to go downstairs and hang out with Gray and Grant.

The incident set Sophie's progress back years. She was suddenly very reactive. When we went to the vet, she was incapable of sitting in the waiting room whereas before she had done well there. She was still panting heavily several hours after the incident, and we were unable to calm her. She almost bit the vet during the exam, which really surprised us.

Our vet reassured us that both she and Sophie were fine. We went home with Sophie's annual exam done, all booster shots given, a course of antibiotics, and a medicinal cream. Over dinner we discussed how to handle the situation, and I agreed that taking her for long walks away from our street would be the best solution for the immediate future. I also spoke to our neighbors across the street about the Golden Retriever and learned that he did not like their female dog but got along with their male dog. While we did not want to have a lengthy conversation with our neighbors at the end of the cul-de-sac, we felt that it was important to document the incident. Three times were too many to ignore. We hoped that this would be the last time for any canine altercations, but part of protecting Sophie meant keeping a log of who did what.

Staying away from our street meant lots of walks in Alms Park and visits to the enclosed picnic area at Lunken. When we were at Lunken, we always had a tennis ball to toss, and Sophie would jump into the air like a centerfielder trying to stop a base hit. Her antics were amusing, but she was really tough on tennis balls. None of them survived more than a couple of outings with her, so I went online and found rubber tennis balls for "heavy chewers." The day they arrived was a Sunday and the weather report predicted heavy rain for the next several days, so I talked DJ into us driving her to Lunken so we could see if these rubber balls were really worth the expense and give Sophie some off-leash time before the weather turned. When we got there, I saw two women sitting at one of the picnic benches.

I turned to DJ. "Hold on. Let me ask them if it's okay for us to bring in Sophie." I started to get out of the car when I saw a dog water bowl right by the entrance. "Oh, fuck. I think they have a dog here. We need to go."

Just as I said that, three Chihuahuas — well, maybe it was two, but for such small dogs they seemed to have an over-sized presence, and a Miniature Poodle came tearing around the corner to the front gate and began barking like mad. They were hilarious in their determination to drive us off, and we started laughing. I mean, who expects to be afraid of Chihuahuas, except anyone who's ever met a Chihuahua having a bad day? Underestimate a Chihuahua at your peril, interlopers.

Unfortunately, Sophie wasn't amused, and she started barking. I turned the car back on and we fled the scene, still cackling about being run out of the park by Chihuahuas. Sophie had to wait until the next morning before the rain came to go to Lunken again and try out the new balls. Luckily, she found them to be satisfactory, though I had to adjust the force of my throw because these balls could really bounce. No one needed a rubber tennis ball going through a window or landing on a golfer.

As for our neighboring Golden Retriever, his people sensibly fenced their back yard and started taking him and their new Golden Retriever puppy on long walks. This was perhaps the best possible outcome because their dog could get his outside time without supervision, but he also was able to walk with his people and get to know the other dogs on our street. We have never spoken about it with them, but we are thankful that they changed their strategy. I wish all dog owners would be so proactive and responsible.

Nineteen

Winnie and Gus

DJ and I were going to a wedding! It was the first time we had traveled without the kids since before the pandemic, and we were incredibly excited. Not only were two dear friends marrying but we also would have a little vacation getaway in my old hometown. However, the logistics of kids and pets and schedules needed to be sorted first. Luckily, our date night sitter was willing to spend the weekend with the kids and take care of the cats, but that left the question of what to do with Sophie.

We briefly thought about leaving her home for the weekend with everyone else, but Sophie was a complicated moving part. If the original sitter fell through, the kids were easily handed over to friends or relatives, and neighbors could watch the cats. Sophie was trickier and given how specialized her care was in terms of needing to be walked yet being leash reactive, our best option was to board her. We had a six months lead-time on the event. Tori, the woman who had initially trained Sophie, had a space open to board her, and this was ideal. She would be with someone she knew, she could get a tune-up on her lessons, and she would be safe.

During the pandemic, Tori had moved the Pawlished facilities from Norwood, Ohio near Xavier University to a small town in rural Kentucky. This provided her more room for boarding and training, and it gave the dogs plenty of outdoor space for romping. Those were definite benefits for her business and her clients, but since her new location was 45-60 minutes away from us, we had not visited yet. On the morning of the day we were leaving, I got all of Sophie's stuff put together: dog bed, toys, food packaged in individual portions for three days, and dog treats. The weather that day started out on the cool side. You could feel autumn in the air after a hot September, so I rolled down the rear right window of my car a smidge, got Sophie into her car harness, and we headed west on Columbia Parkway, crossed the Ohio River and eventually got on the AA.

I was a little worried about how Sophie would do once we got to Pawlished. It had been eighteen months since we last saw Tori, and while we had good reasons to have been absent, my hope was that she would see how Sophie had matured. Expecting perfection wasn't reasonable but maybe there would be a solid five minutes of "good enough." If Sophie had any idea I was concerned, she didn't show it. Her nose was out the window the whole way, and she managed to find a couple of people to bark at in Kentucky, so she was happy.

When we finally arrived at Tori's, there was another client leaving with her dog. I waited for Tori to give us the okay, then I got out of the car and walked around to free Sophie from her harness. "Be a good girl," I whispered in her ear, as I clipped on her leash and then unclipped her safety harness.

She was a good girl, if by 'good' you mean leaping out of the car and then pulling me so hard it looked like I was water-skiing on the gravel drive. "She's happy to see you!" I said to Tori as I caught my breath, knowing that we had just failed our first lesson. Tori gave Sophie all the love and ear scratches and back pats she could want while I went back to the car and hauled in all of Sophie's travel stuff. "It's been a while." I apologized.

"Yes," said Tori. "Sophie was one of my last dogs for training at the old facility before the pandemic. I'm excited to see what she remembers."

I had to laugh. What did Sophie remember? What had we taught her? Here was the expert, and we were the children tardy to class with unfinished homework. "She may not remember much, but she's made big strides at home." I described how she had learned to grab a toy to calm down when she saw another dog walking around outside, how she sat patiently by the table while we ate, how she knew to go to the guest room when we pointed and said "go" and how she sat when we were walking and another dog walked by. It didn't sound like a lot, but these were huge improvements for us.

Eventually it was time for me to leave. I gave Sophie one last hug and ear scratch and waved goodbye to Tori and headed out. As always when in the country, I wished to have that kind of space for Sophie to run around. Chickens pecking, a garden growing out of control, children climbing trees, and Sophie being a dog. It sounded blissful.

When DJ and I arrived in Lancaster, we were ahead of our friends, Carrie and Laura, who had experienced an epic series of no-good, very bad travel and car related mishaps and thus had a delayed start. Our friend, Candy, from the DoCo, was getting married to Mark, and we were honored to be on the guest list. We had known Candy for over eleven years now, and we had followed her journey as she divorced, juggled life as a single parent, went back to college, dated at an age where the choices were slim, and then eventually met Mark, who was a stellar human being and worthy of our friend.

Oh, wait. Based on the chapter title, did you think Winnie and Gus were getting married? No, that would be silly. Winnie and Gus were dogs. They do not even know each other. They would probably never meet. Their claim to fame was that they were both difficult rescues, adopted as adults. Winnie was a Weimaraner Candy found at a Louisville rescue specializing in that breed. Gus was an American Staffordshire Terrier, who had been slated for euthanasia at a St. Louis animal shelter, and Laura had adopted him.

To digress a bit, the thing about cat people was that all of our cats were weird in their own unique and special way. Our conversations revolved around telling stories and having someone say, "You think that's odd? My cat does this!" Whatever "this" may be, it's always even stranger than whatever wacky behavior the previous cat exhibited.

Now, dogs were far more uniform in their personalities and behaviors. For one thing, unlike most cats, all they wanted to do was please humans. The ways that they may choose to please us could be incredibly irritating and annoying at times, but in their minds, if they did not bark at the mail carrier every day, the mail carrier would not leave. Correlation and causation were almost exactly the same concepts to a dog.

Candy, Laura, and I were all people who loved cats. Cats were our jam. Yet here we were, all middle-aged women, who had rescued adult dogs with some behavioral issues. Out of the three, Winnie was probably the least troubled and Gus the most, but that does not factor in all the variables of animal behavior and our modern lives as humans.

DJ, Laura, Carrie, and I were excited to meet Winnie, and see Candy and Mark get married, of course. When we arrived at their home for the wedding and reception, the scene was the typical "pre-wedding" chaos. Guests were mingling, Mark was at the oyster bar encouraging everyone to try the selection, Candy was telling all the guests what ingredients went into her signature drink, The Candy, maybe bourbon and ginger ale? Winnie was running around looking a bit overwhelmed and since I had never met a Weimaraner before, I was not prepared for how big Winnie was. While I wanted to scritch her ears and rub her belly and get to know her better, she had that look of concentration on her face that said, "I am working here."

When it was time for Candy to stroll across the lawn and walk down the aisle in the center of the tent, Winnie joined her, but as Candy started to go down the aisle towards Mark, Winnie balked. Whatever this was, it was not something Winnie felt comfortable doing. A family member wrangled Winnie, and Candy walked down the aisle and she and Mark were wed as the sun set.

After the wedding, when we were stuffing our faces with delicious foods and talking to various guests and meeting new friends, Winnie was far more relaxed. I don't know if the tension of the day had dissipated or if Winnie had discovered that there were about seventy adults and several children, who were happy to feed her bits from their plates, but she was having a grand time being a canine hostess and center of attention when the bride and groom were making their rounds.

The following July, when I stayed overnight at Candy and Mark's, after attending my thirty-fifth high school reunion, Candy, Mark, and I were lounging on the screened porch and listening to the cicadas, and Winnie was dutifully cleaning their new kitten, Minnie Pearl.

"Winnie is so relaxed tonight. I was a little worried before your wedding ceremony because she seemed anxious, but afterwards, she warmed up to all of us. Of course, it didn't hurt we all were feeding her."

Candy laughed, "Right? She had a good time. Funny thing, though. In all the wedding hubbub we forgot to feed her. I think I had asked my daughter to do it, but she thought I was doing it. Thank goodness everyone took pity on her poor starving face."

"Yeah, if I were you, I wouldn't feel too guilty about forgetting to feed her. Winnie was very grateful to all your guests and it was fun to get to know her."

And that was really what all dog owners wanted: to have their dogs do well in unfamiliar and potentially chaotic circumstances. Winnie was a champ.

As for Sophie staying at Tori's when we attended the wedding, we got a good report. Sophie was well-behaved and matched Tori's energy perfectly. We have had Sophie board with her a few times since, and it was helpful to get the training tune-ups, but Sophie was light years more mature now than when we adopted her.

Twenty

How Is That Possible?

It was supposed to be a routine transfer…

Okay, in reality it was just a normal day with cats complaining and Sophie barking and chores being done. So many of our days in this life were like that and we think it's boring until something unexpected happens. In this case, the unexpected was Gray alerting us to a change in Sophie.

"Mom, look…" Gray pointed to Sophie's ear. At first, I didn't notice anything. Sophie's ears always resembled a gremlin's, but upon closer inspection, her left ear was drooping and filled with fluid. That worried me because I had known a couple of people whose dogs had developed malignant tumors in their ears, which eventually lead to the dogs' demise. Poking gently at her ear, the fluid felt like pure liquid with no lumps or chunks. Sophie did not seem to mind the attention, so it probably wasn't terribly painful, but it seemed like another vet visit was in order because the ear did look like it was about to burst.

The vet visit was direct: "Your dog broke her ear."

"What? How is that possible?"

"She apparently shook her head so violently that the cartilage burst. Does she ever shake her head a lot?"

"Yes, every time a dog walks by or she sees a delivery truck."

"Well, it finally caught up with her. Want us to drain it?"

"Please." Silly question.

Our dumb-ass dog had broken her ear. I had never heard of such a thing. No one I spoke to had ever heard of such a thing. Sophie seemed unaware of the entire situation until a fine needle jabbed the swollen lobe and began sucking out blood. She was not a fan of the procedure, but she accepted it like a champ. The vet gave us several different prescriptions and a list of instructions along with a tubular nylon object that essentially acted like a snood and prevented Sophie's ears from moving.

We went home.

Sophie wore her snood, as I called the nylon tube sock, grudgingly. She was too well-behaved to attempt to remove it, but the looks she gave us when we pulled it up showed us that she was clearly displeased with this turn of events. After a week of giving her medication, her ear filled up again, and we took her back to the vet for a second fluid drain. Obviously, she had no idea why she was at the vet or what they were doing, but she was definitely not fond of the needles or being muzzled while her ear drained.

Eventually her ear healed, if you call an ear that was crumpled like wet socks by the pool "healed." One ear was the perfect gremlin and the other ear was a weird, knotty mess that folded over awkwardly. Had Mr. DeMille called, Sophie would not have been ready for her close-up. Between the hairless patch on her back, the lack of front teeth, and her ear situation, Sophie had definitely become a very individual looking pup. There was absolutely no mistaking our girl anywhere.

All these ear issues paid off in an unexpected way as Sophie was now a celebrity at the vet. The dog, who used to shake while waiting to be seen, was now greeted like a rock star and given all the love in the world. Seeing her excitement is a delight. Now if only we could convince the cats that going to the vet is not the worst thing ever.

Twenty-One

No ID, No Entry

In the period of Sophie breaking her ear, we had several other related incidents. One was a complete accident, and it was totally my fault. I had made rib tip risotto for dinner one evening, throwing the rib bones into the trash. Somehow the trash can, which was normally inside a closed cabinet, was left in the open. While I was watching TV in the kitchen alcove, I saw Sophie snuffling around the kitchen floor and chewing on something hard. Something hard that crunched. Like a rib bone.

Of course, we freaked out. DJ and I counted to see how many bones she had eaten — two. We moved the trash bag into the bin in the garage where it belonged and put in a new bag in the kitchen can. I googled what to do if your dog eats pork rib bones because I knew that poultry bones were dangerous. If you don't already know, let me tell you that searching Google for any medical condition was a rabbit hole of terror. Google never answered, "Calm down. It will be fine. Don't worry. Go back to your TV show and pour yourself a glass of wine." No, what Google answered were things like "bowel perforation" and "intestinal blockage" and "obstruction." None of these were words anyone wanted to hear about anything, ever.

Gray was upset, and she blamed me. "If Sophie dies Mom, it's all your fault," she flatly stated with a withering glance in my direction. Thank you, child, for your helpful and reassuring commentary. No, I have not just had multiple scenarios run through my mind where no one ever lets us have a dog again because our previous one ate a bone and died. I still remember the long and onerous search for Sophie; the thought of having to repeat that made my heart seize.

Taking a deep breath, I called the emergency vets and they were totally calm and nonchalant about the whole situation. "Oh, just wad up a couple of slices of bread into pieces and feed her. The bread will pick up any bone fragments and make it easier for everything to safely pass through the digestive system."

My reaction to the emergency vet's recommendation was just like a GIF of a double take expression, WTAF? "So, we just give her some bread and water and keep an eye on her? And monitor her stools?"

"Yes. And call your regular vet in the morning, if there are any changes."

We did not have any bread fresh on the

counter, but in the freezer, I had a loaf of Milton's Multi-Grain, which was our "emergency bread" should we run out and have a huge craving for a sandwich. As an aside, this bread was great fresh, but it also froze beautifully. The pieces don't stick together, and it recovered well as it thawed. I grabbed a couple of slices from the bag, desperately trying to warm them up in my hands and went to Gray's room. Sophie was napping on Gray's bed, and Gray gave me an accusatory look because that was what I deserved. After giving her the scoop from the emergency vet, we took turns feeding bread to Sophie, who thought this was the best night of her life. Rib bones and a midnight snack in bed. What could be better?

The next morning, she seemed fine. Her stool was normal on our walk, but I called our veterinarian just to be certain. "How big is Sophie?"

"She's about fifty-five pounds."

"Don't worry. She'll probably be fine. You can give her some more bread, if you want." Ugh! Of course this was great news that I was thrilled to get, but after all the previous evening's drama, I felt somehow silly for being so worried.

It turned out that Sophie was fine. We all exhaled a huge sigh of relief. That said, if your dog ever ate cooked meat bones, definitely call your vet. Somehow, we lucked out that Sophie's iron gut would hold up and it did.

Along the same time as the rib incident, Sophie started shaking off her choke chain in the house. Why she waited until she had lived here for two years before she started that trick was beyond me, but it was, like much of her "bad" behavior, a reactive response. She would see a dog and if she couldn't find a toy to grab, she would shake her head and because her head was smaller than her neck, the chain would slide off. Most times we could easily find the chain. We would hear it hit a piece of furniture or slide across the floor. We'd glance around, and there it would be. Until one day, it was gone.

The kids were getting ready to walk Sophie, and her chain was missing again. We did a quick search in all the usual places, but we couldn't find it. Since it was late and the dog wanted to go out and we all wanted her to go so we could go to bed, we threw on Sophie's purple, sparkly Easy-Walk harness. That became the go to solution for months. Yes, the chain was missing for months. That in and of itself was not a problem, but the issue was that both Sophie's rabies and registration tags were on that chain. Duplicating them was another layer of annoyance that no one really wanted to face. So, we continued looking for the chain and hoped she wouldn't need the information.

Life moved on. The painters and contractors had finished and DJ and I were rearranging books on shelves, which was a tedious process, but we needed to do it. When we'd moved into our house back in 2009, we had sort of roughly shelved books by owner. If I had 200 books, DJ had 2000. The bulk of the shelves went to him, but that meant that if I wanted to access an architecture or design book or read a mystery or find some 19th century Brit lit novel with fraught and haunted moors, I had to look in many places. We decided to streamline things, donate books we no longer wanted, and put our books in places where they could be easily found.

I had been working in the guest room.

The bookshelf there was a hodgepodge of birding guides, deer resistant native plants manuals, murder mysteries, political commentary, history, humor, and romance novels. Initially we had thought that a hodgepodge was fine because it allowed guests to find something of interest, but it was clear that after thirteen years some curation was necessary. DJ went in to take stock of my work. His worry was that I might be too rigorous in discarding something beloved. He happened to move a basket with magazines in it. There was a yelp from the guest room, and I yelled, "You okay?" DJ came out beaming and held up Sophie's chain.

"Where was it?"

"Behind the magazine basket. She must have gotten big mad at a deer in the backyard, and she shook it off when we didn't notice."

"Okay, but we can't lose her tags again. Why don't we use a normal collar for that and just put on the chain for walks?"

"Great idea. Done!" And it was done.

Within this same period, it was winter. Sophie may not have loved her custom fleece jacket or the paw cream to avoid road salt, but she loved winter. She was always playful in the snow and would scoop it up with her snout and then dance in circles. The word, cavort, was not used as often as it should be, and without a doubt, Sophie was cavorting. Her joy was palpable.

It so happened that we got a winter storm that was mostly sleet and ice with a few inches of snow, which meant that no one was walking their dogs outside of their fenced backyards. We had the entire street to ourselves, and in a leap of faith and trust that Sophie would be good in these conditions, we took her off-leash. She was only allowed to run around on our property, but she loved every minute of it. Once the roads were a little better, I took her to the fenced areas at the park. We were the only creatures within a half-mile radius. I could toss the ball, and she would sprint and catch it.

The look on her face was so clear: "Finally, Mom! Leashes and rules are stupid. Isn't this way more fun?"

While it was possible to train a dog to be unleashed and perfectly behaved, we couldn't trust Sophie that much. Her peanut brain would short out too easily. We could not trust her to pay absolute attention and give the focus necessary to become that dog. Therefore, our free-range time was very limited and when we had our inevitable thaw, it was back to leashes and rules again. We really believed Sophie was safer on leash. Even though she didn't have the bulk of a typical pit bull or the height of a Doberman, her presence always gave strangers pause. Leash laws existed for good reasons, and we thought within the city, public parks, or suburbs, her being leashed was necessary.

Twenty-Two

The Stories of Pablo and Dixie

Cincinnati loved its beer, and aside from a robust Oktoberfest every September, there was a well-attended Bockfest in the spring. One of the events for the weekend was a 5k race through the historic Over-the-Rhine neighborhood just to the north of downtown Cincinnati's Central Business District. It was a beautiful March morning where the Ohio weather gods had conspired to bring sunshine and temperatures in the low 60s: runners and walkers going at pace, friends and families cheering on the participants from the sidewalk, people milling about doing their normal Saturday routine, children playing. The pandemic was sort of over, and everyone in the world was ready to go back to fun runs and stroller walks.

Imagine this scene. A woman running the race noticed a loose dog. The dog, Pablo, was living its best life, running happily through the crowd, tongue out, being free to enjoy the day. Ahead the runner saw a person walking a leashed dog. She noticed the leashed dog reacted to the loose dog bounding up to it. The dogs began to fight. A Cincinnati police officer pulled out her gun and shot at the dogs, which was essentially shooting into a crowd. One bullet ricocheted. A bullet hit Pablo, who did not seem to pause, most likely because he hadn't realized yet that he was injured. A second bullet hit Pablo, and he was killed. One of the other bullets fired hit the leashed dog in one eye, blinding it permanently.

When I first learned of this tragic event, I attempted to reach out to Pablo's owner and the other dog's owner. My attempt was barely a thought formed around potential action when I realized that the entire incident was too raw and incendiary. It was not my place to Monday morning quarterback the course of events between the two dogs. One dog was dead and another was permanently injured in a chance encounter that in other circumstances would have maybe resulted in a vet bill for both dogs and some frayed nerves for their people. The insertion of a gun into the equation changed everything.

Part of what bothered me about the incident was all the times my leashed and reactive dog had been met by a loose dog. Had there been a gun in any of those circumstances, it would be highly likely Sophie would be dead. She looks like "that type" of dog. She's a mutt. She's a rescue. She's got both American Staffordshire Terrier and Boxer mixed into her Australian Cattle Dog genes, and strangers always identified her at first glance as male. Her chances in the Pablo situation would not be much better than his.

There was another aspect of the incident that disturbed me, and that was the casual way the police officer fired her gun at the two dogs as they sparred in a crowded street. She didn't try to tase the dogs. She didn't try to separate them by getting between them. She didn't try to pull Pablo off. She didn't use her baton. Her first instinct was taking her gun out to shoot Pablo. Shooting at Pablo meant shooting into the crowd. To the best of my knowledge, the officer would not have been sanctioned or punished in any way for her choices that day, and if you think she was an outlier and that other dogs fared better, you would be wrong.

I don't know exactly how everything played out that day, but I am convinced that Pablo did not deserve to die and that the other dog did not deserve to lose an eye simply because a police officer panicked. While it was fortunate no civilians were hit because of the officer's decision, everyone who witnessed the incident, including the officer, now had the trauma to process from the images of a dying dog and a severely injured dog.

Pablo was also one of the bully breed mixes, and it did not surprise me that Pablo was killed. The mythology of the "pit bull" overwhelms the facts. There were over twenty different bully breeds, not to mention the various mixes. To call such a wide swath of dogs simply "pit bulls" and then paint them all with the same brush would be intellectually wrong as well as being classist and racist. We could and should do better.

On July 2, 2023 in Lorain, Ohio that scenario played out with a Lorain police officer and a family pet named Dixie. A call had come into the police about neighborhood dogs on the loose. When Officer Elliott Palmer arrived on the scene, a younger family member was holding onto her two dogs, Dixie and another, by their tails as an attempt to get them under control. Dixie, a three year old Labrador-Golden Retriever mix pulled free from her child's grasp and ran towards the police officer. He shot her several times as she ran past him. A few hours later Dixie was dead, and her family was devastated. The Lorain Police Department did exonerate Officer Palmer in September 2023, and the details of the story show that Dixie's family did not have collars on their dogs, which would have aided in them being controlled more easily. Officer Palmer was apologetic over the incident, but there is still an incredible amount of trauma done to the members of the family witnessing Dixie's execution.

Pablo and Dixie share a similar story that is quite familiar, and the emotions around both incidents ran high. Even in fictional stories, such as Old Yeller where the shooting of a dog is a necessity, people become upset. Perhaps our distress lies in the way we view dogs as the better versions of ourselves and it is difficult to think of any other animal that is so routinely personified by so many.

According to research done by Jeremy Smith at the University of Tennessee, police in the United States kill approximately 10,000 dogs a year. The average was 25-30 dogs per day, and this average would be low because many law enforcement agencies did not keep track of canine shootings by officers. Even assuming that a thousand of these dogs were critically injured by an accident, such as being hit by a car, then shooting them was a humane kindness to end their suffering. That still assumes that 9,000 of these dogs were vicious and were directly attacking the police officer or civilian. However, a large majority of dogs were killed by police simply because police could kill them and not face any consequences. Often the dog was killed in its own home because the officers had come in during a stressful event within the residence and the dog was upset. Imagine that your father had suffered a heart attack and when you called 911, the first responders were the police. The family dog would be upset by all the loud noises, flashing lights and strangers in the house. Imagine the EMTs carried your father out on a stretcher with an oxygen mask, while your dog bled out on the living room floor. The same scenario would apply for a domestic violence call, which for many good reasons always had police on high alert. But this time, the dog would be trying to protect the victim from perceived scary intruders. The police would be already stressed to be in the situation, and everything would go downhill from there.

My hope for the future would be a larger conversation around the use of force against animals by police, especially regarding pets in family homes. Obviously law enforcement officers have the stated goal of going home alive at the end of a shift, but the questions around best practices persist. Fido and Snoopy also want to survive the day.

Twenty-Three

Do Corgis Wear Cardigans?

It was a surprise one day in early 2022 when my mother called and asked if I could be a reference on an application for a dog. They were looking at adult rescues from the shelter one county over from their farm, and they needed someone to speak to their character as pet owners. Obviously, I agreed, though when my mom sent me a link for the dog they wanted to adopt I was baffled as to why *that* dog appealed to them. He was a mutt, which of course wasn't an issue, but he looked like a Holstein cow had mated with a sheep and then been miniaturized into some semblance of dog form. His name was Brutus, and he had the biggest head I have ever seen on a dog who was otherwise medium-sized. He had long, white fur with black splotches and a goofy grin. Was he a dog I would have picked? No, he was not. But that's the beauty of people and their pets. There's a person for every pet and a pet for every person. If my parents were excited about Brutus, I was excited for them all.

A volunteer from the shelter called me the next day. We had a comedy of errors because her cell phone had a Kansas area code and mine a California area code, so I initially did not pick up her call. Who would be calling from Kansas? She told me more about Brutus. He was about two years old. He was anxious being in the shelter with all the other animals and was on medication. He seemed to get along with all the cats and dogs in the shelter, and all the shelter volunteers. What he did not like was being in a loud and active place. I feel you there, Brutus.

Then it was my turn to answer questions. Were my parents in good health? Yes, my mom could probably out work all of us at the age of nearly eighty, and my dad had recovered well from his hip replacement and was active.

Had they owned dogs before? Yes. I detailed all the various dogs we had had when I was a kid: two German Shepherds, a Border Collie, a Bull Mastiff, a Pekingese, and two Airedale Terriers.

What was life like for their animals? All of their animals, whether as pets or livestock or some hybrid of the two, were treated with love and dignity. Routine veterinary appointments were made, vaccinations were up-to-date, relevant spays or neuters were done, food was plentiful and good quality, and the animals were all cared for as family.

Were animals allowed into the house? Yes, of course.

Were animals ever tied up? No. In the times when my parents did not live on a farm, they had a fenced backyard or the dog in question was well-trained and did not leave their property.

How did they handle sick animals? If the animal had a treatable illness or injury, it was treated with adequate veterinary care. Animals with terminal illnesses or injuries were humanely assisted across the rainbow bridge.

I am sure there were more questions, but it honestly felt a little like an interrogation. It was a relief to see the county shelter taking the adoption process seriously, but what I did not know was if my answers were acceptable to current dog ownership norms. When I was a kid, there were no "purse dogs" or expensive treatments. Back in the 70s or 80s, given the standards of the day, my parents were quite progressive, but did those standards hold up in today's world where pets were considered children?

So, I was worried that my parents would not be allowed to adopt Brutus. My fears were unnecessary in that regard. They brought him home, they bought him luxurious dog beds, my mom made him a blanket, he had toys. Mom cooked him special dinners of sweet potatoes and brown rice and other things that would not set off Brutus's allergies.

A day or two later, I called them.

"How's it going with Brutus?" I asked.

My mom sighed. "He's the sweetest dog, but he broke the retractable leash. Just bit it and snapped it in two."

"Mom, why did you get that kind of leash? Those are made for Pomeranians, not dogs like Brutus."

"Well, now we know. We have been to Walmart and have purchased another leash."

A day or two after that, I called again.

"How's Brutus?" I asked.

Mom sounded a bit weary. "It's difficult to walk him. He pulled me over yesterday. He didn't mean to, but he doesn't know his own strength."

"I get it. Sophie is the same. I have a lot of tricks to walk her safely. One is that I don't give her too much lead on the leash, if we are in an area where I might slip more easily."

Mom replied in an exasperated tone, which was a hint that I should end the call. "Well, I know that now."

A day or two later, I called again.

"How's Brutus?"

Mom didn't answer right away, and I immediately knew something was wrong.

"Are you okay? He did not pull you over again, did he?"

She exhaled heavily and paused. "We never should have told you about that dog. We had to return him to the humane society."

My heart sank for her and for Brutus. "What? Why?"

"He was chasing the outside cats, and he was not chasing them to play. He meant to do them harm, and they were rightfully terrified of him."

"That's not good. But your barn cats run from everything. They are so skittish."

"Right, but that's not all. Your father had a contractor out to discuss taking down one of the big trees that has rotted, and while he was talking to the man, Brutus came out of nowhere, jumped up, and attempted to grab the man by the neck.

No one was hurt. Luckily, your father was able to see him coming out the corner of his eye and pushed away just in time. I am just so mad. And I feel bad for Brutus having to go back to the shelter, but I did give them all his beds, his blanket, and his toys. Plus, we gave them a detailed written description of all things related to Brutus, both good and bad. They are going to find a trainer to work with him. He could be an amazing dog, but he is not for us."

"Okay," I said. Part of me was relieved that they had returned Brutus and yet, my heart was broken. This was most likely a dog who needed a calm environment and proper training, but he was too much for most people. His odds were not great. There were so many Brutus-type dogs, and largely that was because of irresponsible breeders and irresponsible owners. This was why the animal shelter had asked so many questions of me. This was why all the applications I had filled out to adopt a dog had been so arduous. Too many animals were expendable commodities from the minute they were born, and this was the inevitable result. "It's good that you were able to do all that for him. Hopefully he finds the right place to live once he has some better training. Do you want me to look around on SAAP for dogs?"

My mom laughed, "No, that won't be necessary. It turns out that the shelter director has been bottle feeding three Corgi puppies since they were a week old, and she wants us to have one in a few weeks when it is three months."

"A Corgi puppy? What the hell, Mom?"

"He is the cutest little thing. Just precious. I'll send you a photo."

And thus Taryn, Welsh for storm/wind,

came into my parents' lives.

Taryn was adorable. Seriously the cutest. And if I thought my parents had spoiled Brutus, that was nothing compared to the home they made for Taryn. Did I mention that Corgis were the cutest? Do not fear; it will come up again. Those perky, fluffy ears! That adorable, little fluff butt! That fat, round belly! Those wee legs! The pictures of a sacked-out Taryn, sleeping on his back with his belly open to the world like Snoopy on his dog house! His funny bark!

Taryn was also a puppy, which meant he was a lot of work. For the first few weeks, I'm not sure if Mom ever slept because she was constantly taking him out to pee at night. And she was watching him during the day. As much as they were training him, he was training them. He had a routine of playing fetch before going outside. He liked to chew on everything. He didn't like the rain, which absolutely surprised Mom.

"He's Welsh," she said. "He's a herding dog! All he is bred to do is be outside in the rain!"

Did Taryn like the cats? We don't think he really noticed them. The cats, who lived in the garage, met him and were unimpressed, and the outdoor barn cats were far too skittish in general to play with him. I did worry about my parents not socializing him, as that was my fear about why Sophie was so dog reactive, but they had a neighbor down the road with a puppy and once both puppies had their sixteen-week shots, they could schedule play dates. My mother's disdainful exclamation, "I can't believe I am scheduling play dates for a *puppy*," had me giggling. On the surface, it sounded ridiculous, but dogs were social animals and we people were not social enough.

I talked to Mom and Dad about Taryn. Mom let me know that he had his second coat in now.

"That's good, you see. He was so awful every time it rained, but now he has remembered that he's a Welsh dog and bred to be in wet weather."

"I am sure it makes it easier to walk him. How is he doing with the cats?"

"They ignore him."

"Poor little guy. Don't you have a neighbor who has a puppy that needs to be socialized too?"

"Yes, but that puppy has not had all its shots yet. When it does, we can get the two boys together. Plus, our other neighbors have Corgis and love them. Taryn has all sorts of opportunities. The Damons think their Corgis are the smartest dogs ever, and really, I can understand why."

"Is it their floof butt?" I asked innocently.

Mom sighed. "No! Do you know what Taryn does? He knows when I am upset with him. Now that he has his second coat in, he loves water. So, he has taken to splashing his paws in his water bowl and often will knock the bowl over, which means I have to go and get newspapers to soak up his spill. Then he chews on the wet newspapers and makes a mess."

"He, um, definitely sounds like the smartest dog ever, Mom."

"Wait, I'm not done. The other day, he played in his water bowl, knocking it over, getting water everywhere. He saw that I was upset with him, as I went to get some newspapers. When I came back, he had already pulled his blanket over to the spill, covered it with his blanket, and was all curled up like 'Water? I don't see any water.'"

"See," I said, "he's learning! And it sounds like he has a sense of humor."

I could hear Mom sigh before she even exhaled. "Yes, a dog with a sense of humor. Just what we want."

Twenty-Four

Growing More Mature

There were two open tabs on my browser. Both were for doggy day cares close to our home. I will not even say a word about the concept of a doggy day care, except that it was a brilliant business model that filled a need and yet made my soul cringe a little. Leaving my skeptical heart aside, two things were becoming clear as we headed towards Sophie's 7th birthday. She needed to socialize safely with other dogs and we needed her not to be home all day every day. Eventually DJ would return to his office downtown. Eventually I would want to do more volunteer work or take day trips that were currently not easily planned because Sophie needed her big walk mid-morning, and it was my responsibility to keep her happy and healthy.

I had not called either business yet. The

idea came to me the previous week, and so I did some preliminary research. I was waiting until it felt right, which might be a neurodivergent trait or it might just be that the older I get, the less talking on the phone to people appealed to me.

Ideally this would work out. Sophie would meet other dogs. She would enjoy her time with them and play. She would be worn out and come home happy. That was the goal. All we wanted was for Sophie to be happy. She's a goofy, good girl, and she deserved some friends.

All the incidents of dogs breaking containment and attacking her had made her jittery and anxious. A doggy day care situation had benefits for all of us. I just needed to make those calls.

Procrastination was a skillset of mine. Bursts of activity were interspersed with the slacking that made my generation famous before everyone forgot we existed. I was literally typing this to avoid making phone calls to doggy day cares and if that was not the most ridiculous thing ever, or at least today, then what was? The Embark DNA test that we ordered for Sophie in November had been sitting on the dining room table for six months. The test was finally opened that morning, and I swabbed Sophie's cheeks for the requisite 30-60 seconds. It was now in the mail. The brand promise of the Embark test, aside from user rumors of being more accurate, was that it would connect dogs with their siblings or relatives. If Sophie had a brother or sister out there, and heaven help us all if there was more than one Sophie, they would probably enjoy meeting each other. Again, it seemed silly to focus this much on a dog's happiness, but Sophie deserved it. All dogs did.

One thing that was obvious was how much better trained Sophie was than a lot of other dogs, at least from the perspective of walking on a street. It was a bit of a surprise once both DJ and I realized it. When we compared notes about walks through our neighborhood, we both shared that when encountering other people or dogs, Sophie would sit when asked. She'd stay seated and wait. What was interesting was how many dogs proceeded to lunge at her while she sat quietly.

She'd matured to the point where she might twitch or flick an ear, but she did not lunge or bite her leash nearly as often as she used to. Walks with her weren't necessarily easy. We were always on alert for anything that might cause a reaction. That said, her reactions were fewer and farther apart, but other dogs were behaving "badly." The part that made me both chuckle and roll my eyes was how they were the "good" dogs: purebred and not maligned in the media. All dogs were good dogs. All dogs could be not-good dogs. These two truisms would eventually be accepted.

The Embark results would come. A doggy day care would be found. Taryn and Sophie would meet. Life would go on until it didn't. A few weeks prior to this discovery, a Facebook notification came up that reminded me how Asha got her pancreatitis diagnosis last year. Had we expected this elderly gray lady to live as long as she had? Maybe. Every day with her was a gift, and if visitors to our house were surprised by her makeup sponge kittens or by her insistence on meeting them, that was not Asha's worry or concern. She was living her best life. We should all follow in her example. Meanwhile Detective

Stabler still basically resided in our bedroom, Scout was still learning how to be a cat at the ripe old age of fifteen, and Clive was still an adorable floof jerk.

Since my current procrastination has passed, I made the mistake of reading the reviews of both doggy day cares. Neither made me entirely happy, but the one where the staff sent the *wrong dog* home worried me the most. There were lots of other little concerns with both, but the idea of Sophie going home with the wrong people made me feel queasy. Armed with the information, I contacted the one where no dogs had been misplaced and set up a time for an evaluation for the following week. Hopefully this would go well.

It had been about a week since the doggy day care was contacted. Their earliest evaluation appointment was the following Saturday, so we would drop her off by 9 a.m. and hope for the best. In sorting through my feelings on this, it came to me that Sophie was a perpetual toddler in many ways. The feeling of worry and concern I have for her was very similar to what I felt when my kids first went into preschool. What if Sophie didn't get along with the other dogs? Would she listen to the teachers? Would they understand her? Would it be fun? What if she got in trouble? What if she got hurt? What if she hurt someone else? Yep. Sophie was essentially a third child in terms of her neediness and my concerns for her.

Twenty-Five

Mixing It Up

The Saturday assessment had finally rolled around, and DJ and I had to get Sophie to the doggy day care. As we were driving through Cincinnati, DJ said, "Turn right here."

"I know where I am turning. How do *you* know where I am turning?"

"I think I have been here before."

I glanced over at him, incredulous. "What? Did we have another dog that I don't know about?"

"I am pretty sure it was the cats. When we went to Chicago."

"We have never boarded the cats because we have always—oh wait." I nodded. "When we went to Chicago in 2012, not when we went in 2016. That Chicago trip?"

"That's the one."

149

"Okay, but why don't I remember any of this? Usually, you're not the one who remembers places as well."

I pulled into the parking lot of the day care, and parked.

"Yep, this is it," DJ affirmed.

I looked at the nondescript building with the business name in a big circle and shrugged. "None of this looks familiar. My Realtor-fu has failed me."

"If it makes you feel any better, I don't think you came with me to drop off or to pick up. Remember, the kids were little and I was the one with the SUV at the time, not you."

"Oh, yeah. Right. You were driving the Drunken Rhino. I would have stayed home with loud kids while you carted yowling cats around. Now it all makes sense."

We dropped off Sophie at the site. The lobby smelled vaguely of dog urine, and I could hear dogs barking in the back. My stomach felt a little queasy, much like it had the first time I had dropped Gray and Grant off at their respective preschools. There was so much that could go wrong, and my brain was rapidly processing every possible failure and then tallying every possible remedy. We had come so far with Sophie, and I wanted her to do well, but she was practically quivering with excitement. The peanut brain was very close to shorting out and then all bets were off. Luckily an attendant came and took Sophie, writing her name on a temporary tape collar and taking her towards the barking dogs. With a sigh, I took the Sharpie another attendant gave me to write Sophie's name on her lunch bag, and I was grateful to have remembered to pack her a lunch because the facility had a box to collect lunches. It really was like dropping the kids off at preschool. Hopefully with the lunch and some new friends, the evaluation would go well.

DJ and I didn't say much on the car ride back. We had reached a potential milestone, and in a few hours, we would have a day care verdict. When we got home, it was weird to be there without Sophie. She was definitely our early warning detection system, and she often had a lot to say on Saturday mornings.

Gray and I had gone to the mall for an extended day of shopping. This was a bit of a departure for me, as I viewed retail shopping as a surgical strike, not a leisure activity. However, when the fifteen-year-old wants to shop for spring clothes and look at prom dresses, the universe's rules for this require at least one parent to come along and cheer lead. We had a good time, and I even found some things to buy for myself. It's hard to go wrong in the Nordstrom shoe department. We finished out the day loaded down with boxes and bags, happy to have accomplished our goals.

The doggy day care had not called by the time we left the mall, so I assumed that Sophie had made it through the evaluation, but the trainer had also not yet emailed me the report. Gray and I showed up to collect Sophie and learned that she had been a good girl. She had been somewhat timid and slow to join groups, but she was with little dogs and had fun. They brought Sophie out, and she had the biggest dog grin. She was thrilled to see us, of course, but she had clearly had a grand time woofing it up with her new canine pals.

On the drive home, I noticed that she was a little less reactive than usual. She was just sitting in the middle of the backseat with her smile. Was it just that she was tired or was there something else to consider?

Sunday was also busy, but Sophie managed just fine with her normal walk. DJ noticed that she did not pull quite as much. There was a very fine distinction between Sophie pulling *a lot* and *not-as-much*, and she was not so reactive on the leash.

Monday, I took her to Lunken to play before the rains came for the rest of the week. She remained relatively more chill than she had previously been.

On Tuesday, she had to return to day care because we had a number of events scheduled and could not fit everything in while giving her the proper attention. Per normal, she got strapped into the back of the car, but the minute she realized where we were going, she sat at attention with her huge grin. I dropped her off without incident, and on the way home, I wondered about her behavior. She had not grown up with dogs. She had lived with cats. We'd always assumed that she'd be aggressive with other dogs because she was reactionary on the leash and in the car and at home. Countless people had told us about her bad behavior with other dogs. It was part of the reason why she had been kept in a backyard shed for months instead of with her secondary caregiver's dogs. Yet, I had seen so many pictures of her with other foster dogs, and she was well behaved and happy. We had seen her with the dogs from the one Rover family, and she had done well.

Could it be that she just didn't have the ability to show her interest in meeting other dogs in an appropriate way? Because she was absolutely doing well at day care and she displayed less reactive behavior at home. So far, fingers crossed.

Who was to know? The mysteries of Sophie were vast. It made me a little sad that she could have been in day care sooner if we had trusted her more. Or maybe it was the stability we gave her that allowed her to feel secure at day care. When we picked her up that evening, she was excited to see us as always, but she was also somewhat calmer in the car again. Whatever the reason, she was a champ at day care, and that was a weight off our shoulders. Over two and a half years of daily work had gotten us all to this point, and that was worthy of celebration.

Twenty-Six

CRF'S

Both kids were in the car. It was a Friday afternoon after a long week, and I had just picked them up after school. I was negotiating their demands to *do* something as a family with the knowledge that we had a jam-packed weekend with a bat mitzvah for one of Grant's classmates, a party for that classmate that Grant needed to attend, a Derby Party DJ and I were attending that overlapped with the bat mitzvah party, which added logistical complications, and Mother's Day.

The kids wanted gelato. How they had decided on this was beyond me, but that was where they were in mutual agreement. I even offered to stop at a local creamy whip on the way to get Sophie in the hopes that they could be bribed by expedience but no such luck. We were expecting thunderstorms any minute, and in response, I was developing a sinus pressure headache.

At the day care Sophie was thrilled to see us as always. We got her belted into the backseat with Grant and continued on our merry way home. As we pulled out of the parking lot, Sophie saw a person walking and let out a yip, which was not her normal bark.

"Did you hear that, Mom?" Gray asked from the passenger's seat. "Sophie's bark is different; it is a higher pitch."

I nodded. "It's definitely sharper and higher pitched. You're right."

Grant patted Sophie. "What a good doggo you are with your funny, little bark." He looked at me and asked, "I wonder why she's doing it?"

I shrugged. "Maybe she uses a higher pitched bark at the day care to get the attention of the people?"

"Maybe," Gray agreed. "She is so much calmer than normal, and she has only been twice, officially."

Within five minutes of Gray's statement, Sophie proved that she was not calmer by any stretch. We were maybe a mile from home when she saw another couple of dogs being walked and lost her damn dog mind by barking up an aria. Afterwards, she had just calmed down a little but was still breathing heavily and on edge, when she saw another dog out with its person, and this time, if she could, she would have levitated out of the car. In fact, she was so big mad that she was farting in rage. Right in Grant's face.

"Oh, God. She stinks. Ugh. Sophie, get away from me! Stop it!"

Gray and I were trying not to giggle, biting

our lips to make serious faces, but I broke first and then she followed in a torrent of laughter. We turned the corner onto our street, and Sophie saw a third dog and got all amped up and flatulent again. At this point she was rocketing around the backseat, even though she was still belted, and Grant was basically curled up protecting his face. I waved serenely at the woman walking the large, white, fluffy dog and pulled into the garage and put the garage door down. Waves of laughter were coming out from me and Gray, and poor Grant was in the backseat yelling, "Sophie is rage farting! This is worse than mustard gas. Sophie, what have you been eating?"

We were all finally able to settle and exit the car without further incident. At least we'd made it to the weekend, and Sophie could go hang out with the cats, if they would have her.

It was Wednesday evening the following week when I saw DJ peering at the rag rug in front of the kitchen door.

"What is it? —ewww…gross," was the general reaction of everyone in the house. It turned out to be a relatively large bolus of chewed and partially digested grass. Since we did not have any ruminants living in the house, our first guess was that Asha had finally expelled the motherlode of a lifetime of chewing grass, but upon further inspection, we decided it was Sophie. Because c'mon…once you are a parent of pets and/or humans every excretion was up for further inspection, especially when they could not talk.

"That is a lot of grass. I hope she's feeling better," was DJ's take. Sophie just looked at us like we were supposed to be doing anything else:

giving her treats, throwing a toy to her, scratching her belly.

"Maybe we keep her home from doggy day care tomorrow." I voiced my thought. Sophie appeared completely fine, so we were prepared to forget about it as a one off, until we returned to the kitchen to find two piles of diarrhea on the kitchen floor, which luckily was tile.

DJ took point on clean up duty of this too, as it looked enough like vomit to make me queasy.

"That is a lot of poop," was my helpful comment.

DJ looked up at me and simply said, "Would you please get another roll of paper towels? Thanks."

Upon my return with two new rolls of paper towels because this was not my first do-si-do with assisting in the clean-up of bodily excretions in places they did not belong, DJ came back in from putting the kitchen trash bag into the garbage can.

"It is safe to say that this was not a cat," he posited.

I nodded. "Yeah, that was a lot of poop," I helpfully repeated.

"So you have said. Let's hope there is no more."

DJ did not get his wish. About an hour later I was reading in the kitchen alcove when I saw Sophie squat on the floor and expel two more large puddles of diarrhea. Not wanting to leave her in the kitchen, I yelled for one of the kids to get their father, and then I grabbed Sophie's leash and took her out onto the front lawn.

Sophie looked confused because this was definitely not the normal routine of the day, but neither was pooping puddles on the kitchen floor. She had another, much smaller bout of diarrhea and then wanted to go for a walk. I decided we could do circles around the cul-de-sac, where she was less likely to get into trouble and where she would not exert herself too much. On the third lap, our neighbor Rick came out and we were chatting, since he was going on a business trip to Europe in a couple of days. I asked after Enemy Dog #2, Anna, and her companion, Arthur. Both were doing well. I shared that Sophie was now doing doggy day care and even after four total visits, we were seeing a marked improvement in her behavior, and then I mentioned her diarrhea.

"Oh, Anna had that too this winter. We had to get our bedroom carpet professionally cleaned three different times."

"Oh, no. Poor Anna. Do you know what it was?"

"Most likely something she ate or a virus. She's been fine since."

"That's good to hear. This is probably something Sophie ate as well. Dogs, man."

Rick and I chatted some more, and Gray came outside to take Sophie on a longer walk to the next street. Eventually we were all back inside at home and I was checking my email on my phone when a message from the doggy day care popped up.

"Oh, no. Fuck!" I exclaimed as I read the letter. Phrases like "canine cough" and "strict sanitation practices as regular protocol" and "if your dog displays any symptoms of illness, we ask you to keep them at home until they are symptom free without medications for fourteen days." The last part seemed a bit crazy. Two weeks was a long time, but obviously no one would want to be the plague-bearer. We could manage two weeks away. We had already done two and a half years without help.

Thursday and Friday Sophie was feeling much better. All her bowel movements were perfect, she didn't vomit anything, her appetite was normal though she only got pumpkin puree with a little kibble the first day. She was not quite as active, but we were having a bit of a heat wave, temperatures in the mid-80s. Hot weather has never been her favorite. I took her to Lunken because the park was shaded and she could chase her tennis ball and the actual walk we took was on a table-flat path, so she did not have to exert herself much. Again, I noticed how much less reactive she was. Two Russian Hunting Sighthounds or Borzoi, walked past us as we were playing in the park, and she saw them and did not react. On Friday at 11 a.m., we took a walk past a picnic area where people were having a cookout. Sophie was well-behaved and did not attempt to rush anyone. It was so delightful.

Later on Friday, we decided to call the vet and schedule an appointment just to double check. I had found the inner lining of a ball Sophie had been playing with in the house, and while she seemed to be feeling much better in every way, my worry was suddenly something like a bowel obstruction. While it was highly unlikely, we made an appointment for Saturday morning. It certainly would not hurt to check.

Normally DJ walked Sophie on the weekends. Sometimes I'd join him, but it was often nice to have the free time to stay in pajamas and sip coffee without having to rush anywhere. This

Saturday morning, I decided to walk Sophie myself to the vet. It was slightly less than a mile away, and her 9:30 a.m. appointment meant it would not be too hot outside for either of us.

The same veterinarian, who had drained Sophie's broken ear, came into the exam room with the vet tech. "Do you think she needs a muzzle this time?" the vet asked. I shook my head and said, "No." After a thorough examination, the vet pronounced Sophie to be completely healthy. She ran through the symptoms of kennel cough, and Sophie did not have any of them. We talked about her trash panda ways and the ripped-up ball, but the vet was not worried. Over and over again, the vet and the tech kvelled about how friendly and good Sophie was. Aside from her being extremely reactive the one time she came in because of the Golden Retriever's attack, I could not think of a time when she had not been good, but maybe the vet had a different way of evaluating dogs. It was great to see her shining as we knew she could. Sixty-one dollars later, we were free to go home. Peace of mind was priceless.

Sophie went back to doggy day care a few days later, and we breathed a sigh of relief. Life was back to normal.

A month later, *normal* was kicked in the teeth by a bout of hacking and retching that led to Sophie throwing up white foam. At first, we thought it was allergies because she suffered from them and everyone else in the house was puffy-eyed and sneezing thanks to whatever happened to be in bloom. Then I thought back to kennel cough. Once again, googling symptoms was terrifying, and the list included everything from kennel cough to heart failure. Once again, I called the vet and gave them the symptoms. The person said, "You live close by, right?" and I was able to assure her we did. "Great. Can you be here in five minutes? And come in the side door. We don't want to infect any of the other dogs."

The good thing about dogs, as compared to cats, was that they generally liked car rides. It was trivially easy to get Sophie into her harness and to the vet in five minutes, which made me understand why every time Sophie looked at us sideways, she went to the vet unlike the cats who tended to slink away until they were better. The bad thing about dogs was that they got kennel cough, which was what Sophie had this time.

The vet was prosaic about the illness and prescribed drugs that needed to be taken two times a day. It would be another two weeks symptom-free before Soph would be able to return to doggy day care, and as disappointing as that fact was, I knew that we would be just fine. Compared to where we had been when she first arrived and could not even walk in a straight line going forward on a leash to where she was now, I marveled once again at how far she had come. Even the vet, when told Sophie was going to doggy day care and doing well, was pleasantly surprised. Celebrating how far she had come felt really good.

Twenty-Seven

Canine Conundrums

Sophie's fan club of men with trucks had just added another enthusiastic member. In fact, he may become the honorary president of the club. I know this because he has actually put his tool-box down, sat on the floor, and allowed Sophie… stinky Sophie…to joyfully lick his face.

It had been a good week for Sophie. At least two of our walks involved her getting treats: a biscuit from a landscaper and some dried meat shavings from a custom dog food supplier making his neighborhood rounds. We were stopped ostensibly to compliment Sophie, as was deserved, but we also accepted the company sales pamphlet because we knew the deal. Plus, we had our air-conditioners checked for the season, so the initial visit was a HVAC technician and an apprentice. Sophie got plenty of pats from them.

Unfortunately, one of our units was basically dead. We had kicked that particular can down the road a few years by adding freon at the time, but there was a hole in the compressor or some such and we needed a new unit and yada yada yada.

You will have to forgive me for the blasé attitude about spending thousands of dollars, but the unit had literally failed two years ago exactly one week outside of its warranty period. There were words for that type of situation, but none of them were appropriate for a story about a dog.

Since we needed a new unit, the HVAC company sent out a sales representative, though his business card referred to him as a "comfort consultant." As someone who used to work in sales, I may have rolled my eyes a bit. Anyway, he loved Sophie and Sophie loved him. Of course, that happened. Of course, we purchased a new air-conditioning unit that had a longer warranty and a higher SEERs rating. Of course, we could get the new unit installed the next day.

So, imagine my complete lack of surprise when I returned from running my errands the next morning and discovered that the install technician and Sophie were best buds. He and his co-worker were all about Sophie, but he was particularly enamored. Eventually it came out that he had two pit-bulls and loved them both to pieces. Throughout the day, as he went from inside to outside the house, he would stop to talk to me about dogs while letting Sophie love him to death.

During one of the conversations when we discussed bully breeds and their propensity for food and environmental allergies, he talked about a rash one of his dogs had gotten. What he said next crystallized so much for me, and it made me realize part of why I felt like Sophie was so precious.

"Yeah, my dog had this rash and nothing over-the-counter was helping. She needed to see a vet, but I was afraid to take her."

I must have given him a quizzical expression because he continued, "People want to kill these dogs. And I was worried that if I brought a pit-bull in with something wrong, she would get taken away." The rest of his story had a happy ending because it turned out that in his travels to Colorado the dog had picked up a rare skin condition that was treatable. The shocking part was the course of medication cost $80 per pill, and it was way more than one pill necessary. Still, we both agreed that we would do anything for these dogs.

After he left, I thought about what he had said about human intent with bully breeds, and there was a lot of truth to it. The fact was that these dogs were some of the sweetest, most family-oriented dogs you would ever meet, but because they were also tough, they had been misused and abused as bait and fighting dogs. What happened with Michael Vick's dogs was merely a celebrity-oriented version of what happens every day when people with no scruples use these animals in the most callous and vicious ways possible. On my local crime app, there were daily 911 calls for "loose pit-bulls" and every time I saw those notifications, I hoped that the dog was not given a death sentence. We humans saw patterns and we want to attribute meaning to those patterns and then those patterns become societal "truths," even if the way we had interpreted the pattern was entirely wrong in the first place. This lack of understanding of what we saw before us applied to far more than just dogs, but Sophie was very needy and required this story to be about her.

There was another worry, too. The fear was that Sophie would be stolen. When I mentioned the one doggy day care where the dog went home with the wrong person, it made me physically ill. How hard would it be for someone to say Sophie was theirs? She was an indiscriminate lover of people. She trusted people. Even though she had a bad patch for a few months where she was locked in a shed before SAAP took her in, her outlook on the world was that people were good.

We have had contractors visit the house and eye her, not out of fear but out of avarice. They have been young men working tough jobs for not much pay, and dognapping was not exactly a high-profile crime. That digression was admittedly a bit paranoid, but it was definitely in the back of my mind, even though I was well aware that anyone could walk up to almost any dog rescue organization and walk away with their choice of bully breeds. It was not as if she was a Basenji or a Vizsla or even just a pure-breed anything. She was thoroughly a mutt, a dime a dozen. Yet, she was also incredibly precious.

I was in the guest room, finishing my coffee and planning my day. Sophie was asleep on the bed, pressed against my right hip. Asha was curled up and purring between my left arm and side. Sophie started to have one of her nightmares where she twitches and whimpers, and I put my hand on her back and said, "Sh...it's okay." She immediately sighed and calmed down in her sleep. Those nightmares break my heart. When she first had them, I was worried they were seizures, but they only happened when she was asleep and they stopped the minute I put a hand on her back. Everything should always be good in my sweet girl's world.

After the HVAC installation technician left, DJ said, "He loved Sophie. He even offered to dog sit for her anytime. We talked dogs for a while. He has two bullies and a stray cat he adopted."

"Yeah, I heard about the cat. He brought it in and it comes and goes, but one day he watched it fight two raccoons and win. He was amazed how tough cats are. Scout reminded him of that cat."

DJ cocked an eyebrow, "Can you imagine Scout fighting *anything* and winning?"

"Ha! No. Asha and Clive would do okay, but Scout does not even know she is a cat."

It was later in the day that I made the mistake of reading a local Reddit thread about an incident with two dogs at a park near our house. The person whose dog was injured had every right to be upset. Both dogs were leashed, and the aggressive dog attacked. The owner of the aggressive dog then fled the park with his dog. The owner of the injured dog described the man as white and tall. She described the dog as some sort of "pit-lab mix." The comments were the typical ugly drivel about pit-bulls/bully breeds being dangerous.

First, many dogs were leash-reactive, meaning they were aggressive to other dogs when they were leashed. Sophie had this, and we had worked extensively helping her take walks without incident. We made her sit when a dog walked by and she's leashed. We pulled her to the side and away from the path of any dogs approaching. Ever since the one time she pulled her regular collar off and ditched her leash to attack two leashed dogs early in her stay with us, we used a choke chain, which makes it far more difficult for her to "escape."

Second, everything that happened in that scenario was 100% the fault of the owner. Dogs don't fail people; humans fail dogs. That dog was put into a situation it couldn't handle because its owner did not understand what was happening. Mistakes happen. Humans were human, and dogs were animals. When a mistake happens and it's your fault, own up to it. The fact that the aggressive dog's owner ran away with his dog instead of at a minimum asking if the other person's dog was okay, was a failure.

Third, all pit-bulls contain over twenty breeds. The bully breeds include some of these: Staffordshire Bull Terrier, American-Staffordshire Terrier, Bull Terrier, Rottweiler, Cane Corso, Boxer, Bullmastiff, English Mastiff, Aussie Bulldog, Bordeaux Bulldog, and Boston Terrier. These breeds and their many mixes get lumped into the category of pit-bull, and it skews the perception of these dogs. Imagine putting Poodles with Vizslas with Portuguese Water Dogs with Pomeranians with Chow Chows. It's absurd, but there we were.

The conversation we should be having would be around responsible breeding and ownership. Of all dogs. I was tag-teamed and bitten on the back of my thighs repeatedly by two Jack Russell/Scottish terriers. The Golden Retriever on our corner has literally broken its electric fence, three times as of this writing, to attack Sophie as we walked by their house. We had a Dachshund who lived in our cul-de-sac, who terrorized everyone walking or driving for years. My objective would be not to point fingers at anyone but to clearly state that any dog could be a menace. A dog who was a menace had owners, who needed to do some work to correct the situation because I assure you that unless that dog was trained for use of force or aggression like a German Shepherd or a Belgian Malinois, it was unhappy being aggressive and a lot of its aggression was fear-based. We should actively not put animals in situations where they will fail. Yes, accidents would happen. Mistakes would be made. However, blaming the dogs was pointless and solved nothing.

Twenty-Eight

And the winner is...MUTT!

Due to the pandemic, the Embark test results took longer than the ones from Wisdom. When the email notification finally arrived with the DNA analysis, I was giddy. Opening the email and logging into the site, I watched the video that put all of Sophie's breeds together. Maybe she did have some Basenji? Maybe she was part Poodle? The possibilities were limitless.

In reality, the results did not differ too much from Wisdom. Both had her at 12% Boxer. Embark put her Australian Cattle Dog heritage higher at 37% instead of 25%. She was 21% American Pit Bull Terrier, 17% American Bulldog, and the remaining few percent were attributed to "Super Dog" genes. However, what did grab me was that she had a close relative, named Jackson. They shared 25% of their DNA, so they were essentially half-siblings. I wondered if Jackson's people would be willing to set up a meeting because it would be interesting to see how they acted towards each other. There was nothing else about Jackson shared on the site, so I could not even see if they shared a resemblance.

Sophie had gone to doggy day care on a Sunday. This rare event was because the Premier League was playing its last games of the season all at once, and I didn't want DJ to feel rushed giving Sophie her morning walk. Also, aside from the time we went to the wedding and the time I had visited my parents with just Gray and her friend, DJ had been dutifully walking Sophie every weekend. With me taking her on a walk to the vet on Saturday and with her now at doggy day care, he had a much-deserved break.

When I went to pick her up, the lobby was quiet. An assistant swiped my credit card and called for Sophie to be brought down. Over the walkie-talkie, I heard the person in the day care tell the assistant that Sophie was in the downstairs kennels, not the upstairs play area. That grabbed my attention, and my immediate concern was that Sophie had done something wrong.

Per usual, Sophie came bombing out to greet me, her tail wagging in all directions as she sniffed my legs carefully. The day care manager walked out and with a little trepidation, I asked, "Has she been good?"

He looked at me like I was crazy. "Yes, she's been doing great! She is in with the smaller dogs, and she has made friends with another small dog named Vin. Those two usually play together all day like it is their job."

I breathed a sigh of relief. "That's wonderful to hear. She has not had much socialization and she can be leash reactive."

He shook his head, "Nope. She's doing well. She's been super easy and fun."

"Okay. Whew. I was just concerned because I overheard that she was in the kennels, and I was afraid she had gotten into trouble."

"Oh, no," he said, laughing. "Sunday we like to clean up the play area earlier so we can all go home on time. There are not that many dogs, so we put them in the available kennels downstairs for a little bit towards the end of the day."

"Makes sense. Glad to hear she's doing so well." I gathered her food bowl and grabbed her leash, as Sophie left the building with a huge grin. So far doggy day care was worth the effort because it was making Sophie's life better, not just ours.

A few days later, I was at Growing Trade in Northside to purchase Sophie's raw dog food. The clerk and I got to chatting about our dogs because, of course, we did.

"Thank goodness you have the lamb flavor today. My dog only likes that one and the white-fish-salmon blend. I got her the trout one time, and she refused to eat it. She's normally a total garbage disposal, so why trout is not acceptable is beyond me."

He nodded, "Yeah, my dog is not picky until the moment she is. But she's a rescue. We got her just down the street."

"At Cincinnati Animal Cares?"

"Yeah, they needed people to adopt dogs because they are a no-kill shelter and were running out of room. So, we got this dog. She had been in an abusive situation. She is a total love, except she doesn't know her own strength. She's a pittie."

"Mine's a rescue too. Sweetest dog ever. Mostly."

He held up his right arm so I could see that his wrist was in a cast. "Broke my wrist the day we adopted her. I made the mistake of wrapping the leash around my hand, and she pulled and took off. Took me down with her."

"Ooof. I'm sorry. That is the worst. You're trying to help her, and she does something crazy like that. But it's good you rescued her." I paid for the food. "Dogs, they are a trip," I said, pulling my credit card from the reader.

"That they are. But we love them."

I smiled, "We do. Besides cats are way more finicky. I love my cats, but they are such individuals."

"Hope to get a cat now. The last dog was a cat killer. Maybe this girl will be chill with them."

"Fingers crossed," I replied as I thanked him and left to pick up the kids from school.

As I drove along Martin Luther King Blvd., my thoughts wandered to the ways we contort ourselves to make our pets happy. Bending over backward was not a painful act when it was done with love, but we go to such lengths for our animals yet we expect humans to accept whatever they were given and like it. For the life of me, the way our patience waxes and wanes was baffling. Was it because animals mostly do not talk? Was it because people were expected to know better? I don't have answers, but surely there was enough love and kindness and concern to go around. Right?

Twenty-Nine

Victorious

We were fully into spring, with warm sunny stretches broken by thunderstorms and tornado warnings. One morning I was walking Sophie, and it was one of those perfect days in June where the sun was shining brightly, but it's not too hot. As usual with our walks, Sophie was looking for lizards. This particular walk had some hideouts that the Lazarus lizards preferred, like rock walls and ivy, but Sophie had no luck catching herself any rock candy. The lizards were, as always, too fast.

We had just climbed one of the bigger hills in the neighborhood and were headed for home when Sophie pounced on something she had spotted in low-cut grass. Not only did she pounce, she successfully captured her target: a Lazarus lizard. But as soon as she had it in her mouth, it began to wriggle and she dropped it back onto the grass.

"Good job, Soph! You finally got one. Okay, let's go…" I said optimistically. Sophie had other ideas and lunged into the grass again and came up with her reptilian meat snack once again. At this point, I was feeling a little queasy because normally whenever I have seen these lizards be caught, they manage to drop their still wiggling tail and escape. The fact Sophie had managed to catch one twice was astounding. It had taken her two and a half years to manage the feat, and while I was proud of her for succeeding, the idea of Sophie actually eating the lizard was not acceptable.

"C'mon, Soph. Drop it." Amazingly she did. It was missing its tail, and it looked like it had been chewed on a bit, but maybe it would survive and live to tell its tale to its grandchildren one day. I was pondering why Sophie was successful in this instance, and the only answer I could find was that the low-cut grass made it easier for her to spot her prey. Normally, the lizards would scamper on the rock walls, running out of sight into a crack and then emerging somewhere a foot or two down the wall, while Sophie was still focused on the initial point of entry. This time, she could track the lizard in the grass and therefore she did not lose sight of it. That poor little lizard…

Sophie had no such qualms. She had a huge grin on her face and her steps were light and bouncy. She was very proud of herself, and she should be. Everyone tried to catch those lizards and very few people or animals succeeded. When we got home, I relayed Sophie's tale of triumph to DJ.

He was just as proud of her as I was, but asked, "Why did you not let her keep it?"

I looked him dead in the eyes. "Do you want to go to MedVet at 2 a.m. when it turns out eating a whole lizard was a really bad idea? Because I do not."

He conceded the point graciously, as we both knew that if anyone was going to get sick from eating a lizard, it would be Sophie.

Everything continued apace as we moved into summer vacation. I could drop Sophie at doggy day care and then take Grant downtown to his theater camp. Once home, the amount of free time I had was astounding. It really felt like when the kids first went off to preschool, and I had extended blocks of time in which to clean…or to write…or to deal with contractors uninterrupted…or visit with friends without surreptitiously watching the clock because it might be time to go home and take care of the dog or the cats or the children. There was even time to take a nap, if I dared.

It was impossible to stress how much of a benefit doggy day care was to Sophie. Not only did she come home tired, she had the biggest grin on her face for hours after. It was also a benefit to me to see her happy to see other dogs, see other dogs happy to see her, and to see humans not afraid of her. In fact, even within the short time she had been there, it was easy to see that Sophie was actually a really good girl in comparison to some of the other dogs. None of the dogs were rowdy or mean, but it was clear how very few dogs were perfect. Witnessing those imperfections gave me a little hope. We were not doing it entirely wrong.

As the days got hotter, we were more and more careful with how and where we went for walks with her. We tried to get her out and back before 11 a.m. because several of her breed types were not tolerant to heat. We tried to keep her on grass as much as possible, so that her paw pads would not burn but also because that was cooler for her. We walked in areas with a lot of shade. If she wanted to lie down in the shade and take a rest, that was okay. I also tried not to judge people running with their dogs on asphalt at 4 p.m. when the temperatures had spiked. Did they not know any better? Had no one told them that paw pads can blister and burn? Were they aware that dogs could get heat stroke just like people?

See, that was both the joy and the problem with humans' interactions with dogs. We tended to take our dogs for granted to a certain extent. In the simplest terms, they existed to please us. If we wanted to go running in 100-degree heat, then they wanted to go running too. Like all problems, what we did not know was the real issue. Dogs had limited ways to communicate with us: barks, tail wags, growls, big grins, demanding belly rubs, begging…those were all the basic language skills that they had and that we knew. While there were people who developed electronic ways to help dogs and humans communicate more clearly, there was nothing available yet that could get used at all times and in all situations. Until that time came about, it was our duty to care for our dogs, or cats or goldfish or hamsters, et cetera, to the best of our ability.

Thirty

Dogs Daze and Amaze

Sophie recovered from her kennel cough easily, but she was bored. The weather was unpleasant: scorching hot and often very humid. Our options with her were limited. We went on shaded walks that were barely a mile mid-morning. We took her to Lunken on Sunday mornings when it was not raining or too muddy. She had her other shorter daily walks as well, but none of it was ideal. We allowed her to hang out on the veranda with us and we gave her a few minutes unleashed, but heavily supervised, in the backyard. There just were not many ways to release her energy without current constraints. It didn't help that Grant had somehow managed to pick up COVID. How someone who was spending his summer on the X-Box could get sick was baffling. But therefore, he was unavailable to help walk or play with Sophie. It was not ideal that Gray had hared off to South Carolina on an impromptu jaunt with her friend, and then returned home for barely forty-eight hours before heading to summer camp. The only break we caught was that Sophie remained unbothered by fireworks, so the Fourth of July displays did not upset her.

What all this meant was that DJ and I were left with the care of Sophie at a time when we had many other competing issues going on. The world's ugliest kitchen was scheduled for a remodel in about nine months because after thirteen years in our house, the thirty-year-old kitchen was showing its age. We had valiantly tried to keep the current kitchen as long as possible because neither one of us liked to remove things that were functional, even if they were ugly and did not match the style of the house. It was wasteful and bad for the environment to simply rip everything out and start fresh just to please a current aesthetic, but we were at a point where appliances were no longer working well. It was time for a makeover, but that meant a lot of our time was spent at appliance dealers, countertop manufacturers, and cabinet makers. That meant we had less time for Sophie.

I was counting the days until we could visit my parents for a few reasons. I was looking forward to seeing them. The annual August trip for my dad's birthday was always fun, relaxing, and an opportunity to unplug. Sophie and Taryn could play together and romp around. And when we returned, Sophie could go back into doggy day care to play and burn off considerable energy.

Meanwhile my parents were busy as always. While they had not found a way for Taryn to meet other dogs, they had played host to two older than Taryn, about two and four years old respectively, female dogs, who had just shown up outside the barn one morning. There was a whole kerfuffle with my mother, not wanting dogs digging in her garden, calling animal control and discovering that animal control was closed on the weekends in their county. So, she had called the county sheriff and told that office about the dogs and her concerns for her flower beds and tomatoes. The sheriff had expressed sympathy but had made it clear that there was not much to be done in this situation and also, it was the weekend. Runaway dogs would just have to fend for themselves.

My parents didn't use social media, so they contacted some neighbors to get the word out. One of their neighbors offered to take the dogs, but the dogs then ran off to another neighbor's farm. Those neighbors thought they could keep them, but the dogs managed to escape out of the barn. The older one returned to my parents, and at this point, Dad kind of fell in love with her, a very sweet-natured Labrador mix with lovely leash manners and a good way of managing Taryn. Just as they were discussing the possibility of keeping the older dog, it turned out that the dogs belonged to some people who had a farm just across the county line a mile away. The owners had been house-sitting another dog and all the dogs had been in an enclosed backyard, but their two had escaped. The younger one was found at home, waiting patiently at the door. The owners came and collected the older one. Because they lived in another county, their sheriff's office didn't know about Mom's reports and my parents' sheriff's office didn't know that dogs were reported missing.

Once all the dog drama settled however, my parents decided that an older, calmer female dog, who did not hate cats, would be a perfect companion to Taryn. In terms of having two dogs to alert them to visitors and to have an older one to help teach Taryn and possibly relieve some of his anxiety made perfect sense. He had become very fearful of random things in the past couple of months…the kitchen stove, for example. Mom gave me more of his backstory when I questioned his anxiety, and it turned out that Taryn had been part of a large litter of Corgi pups whose mother rejected them all at birth. The breeder had failed to act quickly enough and two of the puppies had died, but the other five were all bottle-fed from three days old. Taryn had anxiety in part because he and his siblings had not had time to bond with and to learn from mama. Obviously, a patient, older female dog would be helpful, and my parents began a dog search again.

Thirty-One

What's Shaking?

We were in the home stretch to visit my parents. The plan was to leave Tuesday morning and come home Friday afternoon. We hoped to avoid crazy thunderstorms or tornadoes on the drive, but as was typical for Ohio as July slides into August, it was hot and humid. Thanks to the entire do-not-want-to-get-kennel-cough again before seeing the puppy conundrum, the excessive heat limited us to walking Sophie for about twenty minutes each day mid-morning instead of either sending her to day care or taking her on a longer and more robust walk.

It was a particularly brutal afternoon on a Saturday. I'd gone swimming in the morning, and DJ had walked Sophie. The excitement for the walk was that Sophie got to meet a toddler and was very good, and the toddler hugged her and allowed her face to be enthusiastically licked. We were now draped over various pieces of furniture in the living room with cold drinks at the ready and various electronic devices for entertainment.

"So, she was good with the little kid?" I asked DJ as I absentmindedly scrolled through Twitter.

DJ looked up from his soccer game. "Yeah. She was great. And the little kid loved her."

"Awww, that's awesome. She really loves children. I wish we could help her be less enthusiastic about her love for them. Her exuberance is scary to someone the size of a toddler. But when she meets them, if they allow it, she's always so good with them." I looked down to cast a beneficent gaze on our beloved Cheese-Hound and noticed something unusual. Sophie was twitching in a very odd and rather disturbing way.

"Hey, DJ...when you were out with Sophie, did she eat any grass?"

"Yeah, some. Same as usual."

Sophie has always been a grass-chewer. We were diligent about not letting her eat much, but if we were walking on grass and she saw another dog, she would chew on the grass as a way to calm herself. It's not ideal behavior, but it was a huge improvement from when we first got her and she'd lunge, bark, pull and try to knock us down in a frenzy to get to another dog. The worst outcome of her chewing on grass was that she'd sometimes defecate with a long string of poop-covered grass hanging out of her anus, but in general, the little grass she chewed never hurt her.

Additionally, as a sworn member of the

Canine Urination Club of America, chewing grass was a way to both know and to ingest other dogs. We definitely preferred this method of gathering information over the idea of her being reactive and going after another dog. Our experiences with Sophie had taught us that incremental goals were more effective than attempting an entire correction at once. The peanut brain shorted out too easily and then we were left with an unhappy, confused, and poorly trained dog if we did not give her short-step wise training corrections.

This time, however, I was thinking about the hot and dry weather we were having. We live on a street that a friend once referred to as the "most heavily landscaped in Cincinnati," by which she meant that practically every landscaper in the city had a property here as a client. In addition, the lawns were perfectly green, thickly turfed, and weed-free. When we first moved here, we used a lawn care company to manage weeds and to fertilize the front lawn because there had been little attention paid to it for years prior. We also wanted the lawn to be enjoyable for little kids, as that front patch of grass was really the only flat place we had on the property where they could easily play. About five years ago, we had canceled the lawn care service as we wanted to move towards a more natural lawn, which probably freaked out our neighbors a bit. Dandelions and clover, gasp!

The lawn care companies posted a warning on little signs that the lawn had been chemically treated. Children and pets were advised not to be on the grass for the first 48-72 hours. Walking Sophie every morning, I had passed multiple different companies applying weed killer sprays to yards. If our street has fifty houses, forty-seven of them all used lawn services.

Looking down at Sophie, I tried to encourage her to come into the guest room and get up onto the bed with me. She refused, and that had me worried because lying on the hardwood floor against the fireplace in the living room could not have been comfortable.

I glanced at DJ, who was reading a book and not noticing my concern in that moment. "I think she has been poisoned," I said and laid out all the reasons why I thought that.

"I see," he replied, as he put his book down. "What do you suggest we do?"

"I'm going to call the emergency vet in Fairfax and see what they say." Of course, it was 5:30 p.m. on a Saturday. "Why does she never get sick during normal office hours?" I moaned.

DJ laughed, "Because she is a toddler. How many times were you calling the emergency line at the pediatricians when the kids were little?"

"Point taken. Why don't you take her out to pee and maybe see if she will eat something? I am calling right now."

I dialed Med Vet and was put on hold. Eventually my call was picked up. They were very sorry. While Sophie's condition sounded concerning, they were at capacity and could not see any emergency cases right now. The vet tech asked if I knew which lawn service had been used, and I cried despairingly, "There are like ten different companies, and they all have accounts on our street."

"That's too bad," she replied softly. "If you knew the exact company, you could call the pet poison control line, and they would be able to help you. Unfortunately, not knowing which company's product she may have ingested makes it much trickier to treat her. There is an emergency vet in Blue Ash you can call, and we also recommend Grady's Veterinarians, but they are over on the Westside."

I thanked her and hung up.

The emergency vet in Blue Ash was similarly unable to help due to being at capacity. We could drive to their sister location in Dayton, if we wanted. She did ask me to check the color of Sophie's gums and I told her they were pink-ish. "That is a good sign. I am sorry we cannot help you, but try Grady's. They might have room. We are all overwhelmed right now."

I thanked her, hung up and sighed.

The vet tech, who answered at Grady's sounded concerned, "We are almost at capacity. How quickly can you get here?"

"We are on the other side of town, but we can be there in thirty to forty minutes. Is that okay?"

"Yes, that's fine. I'll advise you that the wait will be at least two to three hours before your pet can be seen."

"Perfect," I replied. "We are on our way."

DJ got Sophie ready for the car ride in her harness and then he settled in the backseat of my car with her to provide comfort. I got into the driver's seat, trying to tamp down my fear and upset. Sophie did not need to worry about me right now.

Grady's was located north of Finneytown, and we were able to make decent time even with having to take I-75, which was always capricious. I was familiar with the area having taken Gray to track meets there, and Grady's was easy to find. We pulled into their lot, which had plenty of empty spaces, and went inside to find a pleasant and mostly unoccupied waiting area.

"Hi," I said, introducing us. "We called earlier. This is Sophie. We think she may have been poisoned by weed killer, but we do not know which kind."

The vet tech took our information, and another tech took Sophie to get her temperature and weight. When they returned, she mentioned that Sophie reminded them of one of their regulars, who was also a SAAP rescue. "They look almost identical, and they are both such hams," she said with a laugh.

"Maybe they are siblings," I offered. While I was glad to hear Sophie was being her best possible self for the vet, my mind was reeling too much to think about whether Sophie had family in the area.

We were told to have a seat and wait. Luckily, we had brought charging bricks and some water, but in our rush to leave, we had not considered what waiting would be like for Sophie. The floor was a hard surface, tile if I recall correctly, and the seating was large wooden benches, kind of like church pews, arranged in groupings of three around the corners of the space. I tried to get Sophie to sit up on the bench next to me, but that was not something she wanted to do, and lifting her was almost impossible. We did get her up, and she scrabbled back down, so the hard floor it was.

It took roughly two and a half hours to be shown to an exam room and seen by a tech. It was about another thirty minutes before we saw the vet. All of that to be basically told that there was not much they could do, but they did give her anti-nausea medication. We had thought about doing bloodwork, but by this point, whatever she had ingested nearly twelve hours earlier was mostly out of her system. She was still shaking and twitching a little, but she was much better than she had been even four hours earlier.

I paid the bill of $183.57 while DJ got Sophie settled into the backseat of the car. As we were driving home, I asked him if he remembered when we used to go on date nights when the kids were little. He said he did. I asked him how much we typically spent for the babysitter, dinner, drinks, and a movie or other entertainment.

"About $180 to $200," he replied immediately.

With a laugh I said, "Welcome to our first date night since the pandemic. At least the kids are old enough not to need a sitter anymore."

"Yeah, but the movie sucked."

"Yeah…"

The next morning, I posted the video of Sophie shaking along with a description of events on the SAAP Facebook group. Mostly my goal was to help educate people about the dangers of weed killers, especially to animals. The comments were generally sympathetic and helpful. Someone suggested a basket muzzle for walks to help prevent her from being able to eat grass. Most people offered support because we were all pet parents of rescues, and we knew that rescues are often very much their own "people." There were some negative comments, but as with anything, people had the right to offer their judgment. We certainly had plenty to consider, though we also fervently hoped that there would not be a "next time."

Sophie made a full recovery. We had to drill it into the kids for the 900th time the dangers of letting her eat grass. We had to remind ourselves that while she was a much calmer and happier dog than when we first adopted her, she still had reactivity triggers. As her people, it was our responsibility to keep her as safe as possible.

As with many instances in life, it was on to the next thing after immediately clearing one unexpected hurdle. We needed to pack and prep for our trip to my parents' farm. We had everything done: cats were to be watched by their regular sitter, mail was stopped, outside plants were thoroughly watered. Tuesday morning dawned and we managed, despite sleeping badly and being rushed, to get out of the house on time and to have everything properly packed. I had even remembered to wrap the gifts for Dad and pack his birthday cards.

Once on the road, it took Sophie a while to settle. She's never been an easy dog in the car. She would always be anxious, on alert, and unable to just curl up and fall asleep the minute the car pulls out of the driveway. However, this was a familiar trip for her, and so while she did not break her alert demeanor, she refrained from barking at everything that moved — which happens to be a lot of things when you are in a car, surprisingly enough.

We made our normal stop at the Piqua Dairy Queen, and this time the server brought Sophie a pup cup, which made her day. Within forty minutes we were back on the road. I had texted my parents, asking them to keep Taryn inside the house, preferably in his crate, so we could let Sophie out off-leash and let her sniff and explore first. My parents didn't pay any attention to my text and when we arrived, they came outside with Taryn running loose to greet us.

It had been a long week, and I just mentally shrugged. I told the kids to take Sophie off her leash and let her out. Let the sniffs and tail wags fall where they may while hoping there was no blood bath. There were 50-50 odds about the initial meeting going well, and if it did not, people had received prior warning.

Luckily, I was not even out of the car before I saw Taryn and Sophie joyfully chasing each other around the front yard. With a huge internal sigh of relief, it was clear that they were going to get along just fine.

My parents were a little concerned about Taryn's socialization, and it was clear that he was rough around some edges. He didn't always take Sophie's direct hints well, but she was very patient with him. Usually if he started to annoy her, she would either herd him away from her or she would roll over onto her back on top of him. Both were effective techniques, but Taryn was not exactly a quick student. He definitely had the puppy energy and the puppy lack of insight, both of which prevented him from realizing that he was not being a proper host and his guest was growing weary.

All that said, it was a joy to watch the two of them play and chase each other at full speed around the yard, cornering hard like race cars on tight curves. They definitely wore each other out, and all of our preparation to keep Sophie healthy for Taryn was worth it. Plus, Taryn was the cutest and he allowed me to give him a gazillion belly rubs. By "allowed," I mean he would flop down in front of me as I came down the stairs. So, if I wanted to proceed into the kitchen or out the front door, it was necessary for me to rub his belly and coo about what a good boy he was. No one had any complaints about this.

We were closing in on three years with Sophie. It's a rainy Sunday morning, and we've dropped her at doggy day care, so she could play with her friends and avoid getting wet, which was her least favorite thing.

My hope in writing about Sophie was that readers would consider rescuing adult animals, especially ones who were deemed challenging in some ways. My hope was that bully breeds were given more love and respect. My hope was that humans decided to take better care of our natural environment because it was the only one we had. These hopes may seem overly ambitious and wishful, but I knew a secret. Human beings, despite our imperfections and our hubris, could work magic when we try. Humanity had achieved so many wonderful things; I had to believe we could do this too.

Thirty-Two

Long Time Coming

The popular theory, known as the Law of Universal Cat Distribution, essentially said that whether or not you wanted a cat, whether or not you liked cats, the universe would gift you with a random one. Now you had a cat. Whether it was a story of a kitten in an engine block or a pregnant mama cat making her birthing nest underneath someone's porch or a stray cat just hopping through an open window and making itself at home, there was no denying the fact that when the universe gave you a cat, you really had to take it.

Asha was that cat for us. She was the perfect cat in so many ways: loving, well-mannered, able to set boundaries without aggression, good natured with all. We knew that we had hit the jackpot with her, and every day since her initial

IBD diagnosis, we had known that we were lucky to still have her with us.

In mid-January of 2023, we took both Asha and Scout to the vet for routine checkups. The vet asked if we wanted any vaccines for Asha and we said no. She was not likely to contract rabies or any of the other diseases that affect felines. We agreed that Asha could continue on as she always had. The vet also suggested a new drug for Scout that was a monthly shot to alleviate her arthritis pain. Since Scout had become increasingly uncomfortable looking recently, we agreed to try it.

In early February, we noticed that we needed to roust Asha to come for dinner and that she wasn't finishing her dinner as often. She also spent a lot of time sleeping on heating vents or sleeping on the heating pad in DJ's office lounge chair. Most distressingly, she no longer cleaned herself after using the litter box. Asha had always been fastidious about grooming herself, and this was not a positive sign. She also could no longer jump up onto anything. We had to pick her up and gently place her wherever she wanted to be.

DJ and I were both distraught, but DJ was insistent that she was purring and still participating in daily life. I knew that he was going to have a very difficult time dealing with Asha's transition into the next realm, but it was painful to watch our beloved cat not even care about her make-up sponge kittens anymore. During a Sunday phone call, DJ's mom suggested that we take Asha to the vet and get her a pain shot. DJ made the appointment early Monday morning and we were at the vet's office that afternoon.

Somehow the vet's office had scheduled the appointment as a "quality of life" visit, so my guess was that they were used to pet owners being reluctant to have the responsibility of ending their pet's life. The vet was extremely kind and thoughtful. She also sighed audibly in relief when we asked about in-home euthanasia services and suggested a company she had used and liked.

It was my job to research the pet hospice/end-of-life service veterinarians. We knew that we wanted Asha to die peacefully with us holding her and then allow all the animals to sniff her once she had died, so they would not be confused as to what had happened. I cannot tell you how scheduling my pet's death almost broke me. Plenty of animals had died in my life, but usually they died from old age on their own or they were hit by a car. Setting an appointment for euthanasia was a surreal feeling, but the hospice vet's office was very comforting and made the process as smooth as possible.

This was February 13th. The earliest they could come out, when everyone would be home, was February 15th. We spent the next forty-eight hours in this very subdued interstitial space, where we knew Asha could die at any moment, but we were waiting for the hospice vet. If we had any doubts about our decision, it was clear by Valentine's Day that this was the right thing to do. I spent the afternoon of the 15th lying on the foyer floor, with one hand gently stroking Asha as she slept on a little pillow nest we had made for her. We had put her little nest against a bank of windows and had opened a vent window near her so she could smell the air and listen to the birds. I was not certain she actually noticed.

The hospice vet arrived shortly after 5 p.m. Of course, Sophie had to greet her, but she was very focused on Asha and agreed that it was time for her to transition. I was not sure Asha was ever fully conscious that afternoon, and I was certain she felt no pain. DJ held her on his lap, and she was wrapped in a towel. The vet also put a pee pad with the towel, saying that it was common for pets in their final moments or shortly after death to urinate or defecate. Within thirty minutes of the vet arriving, Asha was dead.

It fell on me to carry Asha around to the other animals and the children. The kids had said their goodbyes to her when the hospice vet had first arrived, but it was interesting how all the animals reacted. Both Sophie and Scout sniffed Asha's head and then gently licked it. Both Clive and Deets sniffed her and hissed while backing away.

The vet wrapped her in a blanket, put her into a basket on the front seat of her car, and it was over. The next day the crematorium delivered Asha's ashes in a pretty wood box that was engraved "Asha Greycloud." While I missed her tremendously, my major reaction was relief. Watching her be in pain and failing, when she had been such a capable cat until a few weeks before her death, was heartbreaking. We have noticed how much quieter the house was without Asha. Apparently, her near constant stream of burbles and merps had simply become part of the household's auditory fabric, and it was not until she was gone that we realized how present she had been.

Thirty-Three

To The Rescue!

A neighbor at the top of the cul-de-sac had gotten for their kids a little black pug named Penelope. Gray and Grant had discovered her addition to the neighborhood dog cohort when she was a puppy playing outside in her front yard. Penelope was often out, tied to a lead, in the evening when the kids walked Sophie. Gray, being an animal lover, took to Penelope and introduced her to Sophie early on. Blessedly Sophie did not eat Puppy Penelope and they became casual dog friends in the sense of sniffing each other hello, but their interactions beyond that were nonexistent.

One evening I was walking Sophie because Gray was in France on a school trip, and it seemed like Grant had barely gotten her out of the house before returning and claiming she had not pooped. The weather was perfect; a cool and clear evening in late May where many things were still in bloom, and it was not dark yet even though it was close to 9 p.m.

Sophie and I walked past Penelope's house, and she was out on her lead. I chose not to stop because it was getting late, I wanted Sophie to take a longer walk, and distractions were not welcome. Penelope barked at us. Sophie turned her head to see her, but we kept going.

On the return trip, we once again walked by Penelope and we were two houses down when I heard a racket behind us. Turning around, I saw Penelope careening towards us as fast as her short little legs could carry her while one of her children sprinted behind her, yelling her name. Sophie turned just as she ran up to us, and they both casually sniffed each other. Sophie gave her a little lick on top of her head, and Penelope was happily sniffing Sophie's undercarriage. At this point, Penelope's boy child reached us and panted, "Penelope!" which caused Penelope to rocket out from under Sophie and start sprinting around the neighbor's yard.

In order not to add to the chaos, I had Sophie sit, which she did. Penelope would swing up towards us and I'd try to grab her and then she'd veer off in another direction, her child racing around always two steps behind. It was getting darker, and I was tired. The poor kid was doing his absolute best, but Penelope was having the time of her life and was extending her circuit to include houses on the other side of the street. At that point, my worry was about cars coming in or out of the cul-de-sac. Penelope was dark, tiny and fast. If she darted into the street unexpectedly, any number of bad things could happen to her, her child, or us.

And that was when I had a rare flash of genius. Sophie was a third Australian Cattle Dog. She loved to herd us. Would she herd Penelope?

I couldn't risk taking Sophie off leash, but I let the leash go slack and Sophie stood up and was alert. The next time Penelope came by to greet Sophie, Sophie followed her and nudged her in our direction. Then Penelope would leave but come quickly back, and Sophie would nudge her towards her house. It helped that I was walking in that direction at this point. Rinse and repeat with Penelope coming closer with each return and Sophie nudging her more in the direction of home until Sophie had Penelope on the side of the street where her house was and Sophie was nudging her towards the front door.

"Is your front door unlocked?" I asked Penelope's kid.

"Yes," he replied a bit breathlessly.

"Go open it. Penelope will go in."

He did as I said and luckily, Penelope did what I had hoped. She went right in the house. I waved to the kid's mom, the front door closed, and Sophie and I headed back home. The grin on Soph's face was extraordinary. She was so happy to have been useful, and when we returned home, she received a dog biscuit in addition to her regular leftovers from the cat food plates.

We humans forget how we carefully bred wild dogs to become faithful servants. At some point we began seeing dogs as accessories, not as sentient beings with their own needs and wants. Sophie was a dog, who wished to herd and to guard. She excelled at these duties, even though her determinations about what to herd or who to guard were not always accurate. I could not imagine Sophie living in an apartment or not being exercised fully on a regular basis. In fact, the negative that many rescue centers used to deny us a dog was our lack of a fenced backyard. Yet I would argue that the lack of a fenced backyard necessitated us socializing Sophie more; she had to walk on a leash, get over her extreme leash reactivity, learn to socialize with other dogs, and learn when her guard dog instincts were needed. If we had been equipped with the fenced backyard, we would have had an extremely reactive and extremely unhappy dog. That said, there are plenty of times where I wish we could just let Sophie outside to safely play, but it was clear that Sophie would not be the dog she was today if we had only kept her fenced.

Thirty-Four

This Or That

Trust was a component in any good relationship, whether it was with a human or any other living creature. Skilled equestrians, for example, developed a sense of trust with their horses and knew where their mount would excel and where their mount's abilities were less keen. Horses also learned to trust their riders, and good riders paid attention to the signals they received from their horses. Horses, ponies, mules, and donkeys were very in tune with their environment in ways most people were not, and it made sense for us to heed their warnings. We ignored them at our peril.

The need to trust wasn't limited to what equestrian's face. We trusted all the animals we interacted with to behave as we expected. Normally they do. When they don't, we pay attention.

Building trust with Sophie was a slow

process in some ways. Oh, we loved her, but her peanut-brain could short out at the slightest distraction and then chaos would erupt. Whether it was Sophie bouncing around in giddy excitement and ricocheting off people, cats, and objects like a ping pong ball or Sophie seeing a dog walk by the house and that caused her to bark like our lives depended on it, we were not sure for a long time that she had the capacity to listen to instructions in an unfamiliar situation.

Little by little, we eased into trusting her. Small steps. We let her play in the front lawn unleashed after an ice storm. We put her tagged collar on and let her roam around the backyard with us without her leash. We took her to my parents and let her off-leash in the hopes she would know to stay with us in an unfamiliar place when she had only lived with us for a little over a month. All this played a part in building that trust. We trusted her with the cats, even if some of the cats were insulted that we would do so. We trusted her with guests. We trusted her to meet all the delivery drivers, especially her UPS boyfriend, Brandon. We trusted her to listen.

Sometimes I felt a little bad for how long that trust took to build completely. In fairness to us, Sophie was not perfectly trained when we adopted her and our training of her was more haphazard than we would have liked. Our biggest fear was always around her dog reactivity, especially when she was leashed. Being responsible pet owners meant being concerned for our safety, her safety, and the safety of everyone in our orbit.

Doggie day care had really helped Sophie and after a year of going two to three days a week, she was much more chill on leash around dogs. I suspect she knew that her fun times with her dog friends would be restricted if she went to day care and behaved foolishly. That better behavior on leash also translated … somewhat … to her walks, which was an added benefit.

'The essence of life is contradictory. We are supposed to live in the moment, yet we are deeply affected by the past as we anticipate the future.' As I wrote this, Sophie was lying down in the foyer with her front paws daintily crossed as she quietly surveyed the —. All havoc broke out as a UPS truck drove by and parked in front of our neighbor's house. Sophie was waiting eagerly for our regular UPS driver, Brandon, to stop at our house. On this afternoon, he did. He stepped down from his truck and strode across our lawn carrying a case of wine, and Sophie's tail spun in a circle. Her face was in a huge grin. I did a quick survey of the cul-de-sac to make certain none of the "enemy dogs" were outside. Then I opened the front door. Brandon handed me the box and then immediately began loving on Sophie. It didn't hurt that he had a treat for her, of course.

This turn of events took a few years to develop. Sophie always stood with her front paws on the foyer windowsill and vigorously announced the presence of anyone on our property or passing by. Normally her antics would get her sent to the guest room or told to go downstairs because that was the only way to calm her, but one day she slipped past me as I opened the front door, and I yelled to Brandon, "She's friendly!" as he set our package on the steps and allowed Sophie to lick him to death. It turned out that he's a fan of "pitties" and has had two. There must be something about him that she really adored because only our family friend, Pete, received such a ridiculously warm welcome every visit.

The friendship between Sophie and Brandon grew. If we were out walking and he was in the neighborhood and had a stop for delivery as we're nearby, he'd give her a treat and a head scratch before getting back into his truck. She knew the sound of his truck and would recognize its engine when it was a few streets away, which always led her to eagerly wait by the front door. The saddest part was when the driver wasn't Brandon or there were no deliveries for us; she was so dejected and just laid with her head on her paws in the foyer and pouted. Oh, she'd accept a treat from another driver, but you could tell she was just doing it to be polite.

Sophie started out as Gray's dog, and she still was, in large part. But Sophie had spent more time consistently with me throughout the days, and I was the one she looked to first for direction. The hierarchy was me, Gray, DJ, and then Grant, but the levels between each of us were not that deep. Grant, who did not want a dog at all, would now walk Sophie by himself at night and let her sleep in his bedroom when his older sister wasn't home. Sophie would watch movies companionably with him in the family room, and he would play with her without being asked if she seemed bored. DJ, who was most reluctant to add a dog to the family, would sit next to her and feed her little treats while he's reading or watching a soccer match on TV. Sophie was part of the family now, not just "Gray's dog."

As I sat writing at the kitchen planning

desk, while Sophie was asleep and snoring on her dog bed in the alcove, it occurred to me that Sophie and I were a lot alike in some ways. We were both sturdy and stubborn. We loved hard and tended to be prepared to like everyone at least a little. We liked long walks in the woods and taking afternoon naps. We could both hold a grudge, but we were willing to forgive. Was Sophie the dog I would have chosen for myself? I couldn't say. Would I have been the person she would have bonded to immediately? Probably not, especially as I was not a man, who smoked, wore work boots, and drove a pick-up truck. But here we were, a family: people, cats, and an unlikely dog.

We were just short of the fourth-year anniversary of Sophie's adoption from SAAP. Much like people cannot imagine how parenthood would change their life until they experience it fully, it was difficult to remember life before Sophie joined our family. Certainly, the back of my car didn't look like a pack of rabid raccoons had attempted to bite their way outside to freedom. Certainly, if the weather was nasty there was no need to go outside. Certainly, the cats were all equal in hating each other without the threat of a dog uniting them. Certainly, Gray and Grant were occupied in trying to find the most interesting, i.e., difficult to care for, pets.

And then we walked through that glass door at SAAP before Sophie could barrel through it, and everything was immediately different. The cats would probably like a word about these changes, but for all the rest of us, we were better for having Sophie in our lives. In the nearly four years we have had her, we had learned that she was extremely good-natured. She loved us without reservation. She was willing to learn, but we had to learn the best way to teach her. She was goofy, energetic, and sweet. Her farts were foul, her love of baths was non-existent, her snores were deep, and her destruction of tennis balls was unparalleled. There was nothing better than snuggling with Sophie on a cold morning, especially on those laziest of mornings with no expectations for the day ahead. Our world had expanded exponentially with her in our lives. She taught us about unconditional love in ways we did not expect.

Much like everyone had an opinion on how to care for children, everyone had an opinion on how to care for dogs. You would note that people's opinions on cats were not added to this mix because everyone who had ever had a cat, particularly an adult rescue, was well aware that they did not own the cat. The cat deigned to exist, and our job was to serve it. We carried that philosophy into how we acclimated to Sophie to a certain extent because getting to know an animal means gaining its trust. But the canine nature was rooted in obedience. Sophie needed rules and structure, and our job was to get to know her well enough that we could provide what she needed in a way she would understand.

We were a family of animal lovers. I grew up on a farm and always had cats and dogs and horses, but at times there were chickens, ducks, a cow, and a goat. Nature out in rural parts was super shy of humans. We saw more wild animals up close in our Cincinnati neighborhood than I ever saw in western New York or the Hocking Hills of Ohio, but the lessons I learned from a young age were to not fear animals, wild or domesticated. DJ grew up in a household full of cats, dogs, and guinea pigs. His father taught him to love nature and birds. His mother taught him to love rescues.

Some people like to say that animals were stupid, but if you spent time with them you'd realize that was not true. Animals may have trauma from the past that they were coping with in their present. Animals may be put into environments that were unfamiliar. Animals may have a more high-strung temperament. Animals may never have been trained to certain expectations. Animals may simply not be understood because our methods of communicating with them were not always effective. No animals were stupid. Everything I just said in this paragraph about animals? It also applied to humans.

Basically, I would implore everyone to lead with love and kindness. That doesn't mean no rules or no boundaries. It does mean treating everyone else, from your hamster to an elephant, with dignity and respect. It means treading lightly on this Mother Earth. None of us get out of here alive; that's another contradiction in life. We knew we were going to die. I don't care if you call it karma or energy or faith or empathy. Whatever you call it, practice it with positive intent.

I am not a dog trainer. I am not an animal behaviorist. There may be many people who critique our approach to integrating Sophie into our family, and there was nothing I can say about that. We may have made mistakes. We may not have tried every technique. We may have done Sophie a disservice by not fencing our large, yet mostly unfenceable yard. That said, we loved and cared for Sophie every minute of every day. The dog we adopted on October 15, 2019, was the same dog we had today, only better because 'we know her and she knows us.' Ultimately, the question could be asked about who was rescued and who needed rescuing? We knew that answer.

Our family had settled into a routine that was easy and pleasant for all of us. Detective Stabler may still wish that Sophie did not exist, but nearly four years into Sophie's residency, Deets was more resigned than hostile to her presence. Scout and Clive basically did not stress about Sophie. DJ and Grant loved her. Our household was at a truce, if not exactly at peace.

As I finished writing this, Gray sachayed into the kitchen with that look on her face that told me she wanted something and she was willing to argue for it. "Yes?" I asked her with some trepidation, leaning back on my exercise ball "chair" at the planning desk. "What is it?"

She smiled and then blurted out, "We should get chickens!"

Acknowledgments

While these are in no particular order, I have to start with DJ. Without his patience and support, Loving Sophie would never have happened.

Much love to Gray and Grant. You are amazing. Keep shining brightly.

Much love to my parents, extended family, and in-laws. In many different ways, I would not be here without you.

The people at SAAP (Stray Animal Adoption Program) from the management to the foster families to the transport volunteers to the various behavioral trainers, vets, and others... thank you for everything you do.

A specific shout out to Tori at Pawlished. While Sophie will never not be wildly exuberant, Tori helped her learn how to appropriately harness her energy.

Thank you to Animal Hospital of Mt. Lookout Square, MedVet, Grady Veterinary Hospital, and PetSpot. Having safe havens for both medical care and boarding are blessings.

A posthumous thank you to Heather Hamilton Armstrong, aka "Dooce", for creating a community that still maintains strong bonds across the world and for teaching me the value of writing honestly.

An epic thank you to all the wonderful friends I have made from the DoCo. Without your wisdom and humor and excellent advice, I would not be the person I am today. You are loved beyond measure.

A huge shoutout to Jessica, who had an idea and came to me with it. We have done good work.

Many thanks to my dear friend, Candy, who both found me a job and an editor. When I wasn't even looking for either…but somehow she knew what I needed.

Many thanks to my dear friend, Rebecca, who has been alongside me every step of the way from DoCo kitties to adopting Sophie. Your humor and perspective are both priceless to me.

Such deep appreciation goes to all the people, who agreed to read the first finished version of Loving Sophie. And I am giving my utmost gratitude to those, who finished and critiqued it: My parents, Dawn Akemi, Richard Crockett, and Jennie Karn.

Academic acknowledgement to Jeremy Smith, University of Tennessee, Doctoral Dissertation May 2021: "The "Puppycide" of Policing: How The Law Rationalizes The Police Killing of "Dangerous Dogs". His insights into the breadth of these incidents helped give statistical information to an issue that is not fully tracked or researched nationally.

Thank you to both James Estes and Crystal Sands for choosing me to write for your publications. Those writing credits might have been twenty-five years apart, but your trust in me was priceless.

A big Sophie circle tail wag to her UPS boyfriend, Brandon.

Thank you to Joanne Tailele, Jill Yris and Robin Ludwig at Simon Publishing LLC for helping to bring Loving Sophie to life.

"With gratitude to Lisa Binns at Second Shot (501c3) http://www.secondshot.pictures for her fantastic photos of Sophie on the front and back covers and for all the work she does to help pets find their furever families."

And finally, thank you to everyone who gave Sophie any love, including her original family. This sweet girl deserves all the hugs, ear scritches, and belly rubs in the world.

About the Author

Having grown up on two different farms (a working vineyard in the Finger Lakes region of New York and a family farm in the Hocking Hills region of Ohio), Lessa Clayton has a deep love for all the natural world, with the possible exception of stink bugs. As an adult, she attended The Ohio State University in Columbus and earned a BA in English and then promptly moved to Washington, DC where she ended up as a claims adjuster for a local auto insurance company.

Eventually hitting her first mid-life crisis at twenty-seven, she returned to Ohio to pursue coursework to apply to medical school, but fate had other plans for her and she ended up in Los Angeles, California. The creative energy of the city energized her, and she found careers in both advertising sales and real estate. She also married, had children, and bought a house, which were all things she never previously had anticipated doing.

Returning to Ohio over a decade ago, she and her family now make their home in Cincinnati. Unexpectedly falling in love with her adopted city and attempting to remain relevant as a now stay at home mom, she picked up writing again, focusing on politics and issues of social justice. In a surprise to everyone, including herself, she then sat down and wrote a book about adopting an adult rescue dog. Stranger things have happened in the world, but this is her strange thing.